JOHN BUCHAN'S
COLLECTED POEMS

Other poetry from Scottish Cultural Press

Scottish Contemporary Poets Series
(for further details of this series please contact the publishers)

Gerry Cambridge, *The Shell House;* 1 898218 34 X
Jenni Daiches, *Mediterranean;* 1 898218 35 8
Valerie Gillies, *The Ringing Rock;* 1 898218 36 6
Kenneth Steven, *The Missing Days;* 1 898218 37 4
Brian Johnstone, *The Lizard Silence;* 1 898218 54 4
Siùsaidh NicNèill, *All My Braided Colours;* 1 898218 55 2
Ken Morrice, *Talking of Michelangelo;* 1 898218 56 0
Tom Bryan, *North East Passage;* 1 898218 57 9
Maureen Sangster, *Inside/Outside;* 1 898218 65 X
Anne MacLeod, *Standing by Thistles;* 1 898218 66 8
Walter Perrie, *From Milady's Wood;* 1 898218 67 6
William Hershaw, *The Cowdenbeath Man;* 1 898218 68 4

News of the World: Last Poems, Maurice Lindsay; 1 898218 32 3

Canty and Couthie: familiar and forgotten traditional Scots poems,
Anne Forsyth (ed); 1 898218 04 8

From a Gael with no Heartland, Alan McLeod; 1 898218 62 5

The Meaning of Mallarmé: A Bilingual Edition of his *Poésis*
and *Un Coup de Dés,* Charles Chadwick; 1 898218 29 3

JOHN BUCHAN'S
COLLECTED POEMS

edited by
Andrew Lownie
and
William Milne

SCOTTISH CULTURAL PRESS

To our families

This selection first published 1996
Scottish Cultural Press
PO Box 106, Aberdeen AB9 8ZE
Tel: 01224 583777 • Fax: 01224 575337

Poems and Fragments copyright © 1996 Lord Tweedsmuir
This selection copyright © 1996 Andrew Lownie & William Milne
Introduction and all editorial matter copyright © 1996 Andrew Lownie & William Milne

British Library Cataloguing in Publication Data
A catalogue record for this book is available from the British Library

ISBN: 1 898218 47 1

Printed and bound in Great Britain by
Cromwell Press, Melksham, Wiltshire

Contents

Acknowledgements

The editors gratefully acknowledge the assistance of the following:

Alastair Stevens, Strathtay; Anne Stonehouse, editor of the *John Buchan Society Journal*; Bodleian Library, Oxford University; Brasenose College, Oxford University; Browne University, Rhode Island, USA; Cambridge University; Iain MacIver, Assistant Keeper National Library of Scotland; Janet Adam Smith; John Buchan Centre, Broughton; Kenneth Hillier; King's College Library, Aberdeen University; Lord Tweedsmuir; Roy Court, Bannatyne Books; Russell Paterson, Secretary of the John Buchan Society; Stewart Renfrew, Archivist, Queen's University, Ontario; The English Association; The Trustees of the National Library of Scotland; Queen's University, Kingston, Ontario; Hon. William Buchan; Kate Love, Chairman, John Buchan Society.

In addition, a tribute is paid to the *Collector's Bibliography* of Robert G. Blanchard, *The First Editions of John Buchan* (1981), which has been of considerable assistance in identifying the chronology of the various publications containing poetry.

Addendum

Two poems have been found in Janet Adam Smith's papers in the National Library of Scotland. They take the form of letters to Stair Gillon, a friend of Buchan's from Oxford University days.

Glasgow University Library have supplied a copy of a poem which appeared in the *Glasgow University Magazine,* 26 January 1898.

South Africa Poems

Buchan went out to South Africa in September 1901 as a Private Secretary to the High Commissioner Lord Milner where his primary job was to organise Land Settlement after the Boer War. The second poem refers to a plan for Gillon to join Buchan in an attempt on the unclimbed north-eastern buttress of the Mont aux Sources in the Drakensberg, a trip which had to be cancelled when Gillon failed his Bar finals.

J B to Stair Gillon *(1902)*

May 8, 1902, High Commissioner's Office, Johannesburg.

Dear Stair, a scribble frae your pen
Delights me weel, as fine ye ken,
Forwandered in the but-and-ben,
They ca' Transvaal,
A land o' Jews and neeger men,
Nae guid at all.

I'm blith to hear frae freend like you
How blows the wind ower Sgor-an-Dubh,
And sairly that black day I rue,
When first I came
Far far frae a' folk guid and true
Across the faem.

Some day, my man, I'll traivel back,
And we'll set out on our auld track,
Our mutchkins in our pouch, our pack
Upon our shoulders,
And we will hae a fine lang crack
Among the boulders.

We'll climb the hills o' Lorne and Skye,
We'll let nae piece o' rock gang by.
And syne we'll drink Loch Laggan dry
With just a gill
Of mountain dew, the real Mackay,
To fend the chill.

Ye say ye're gettin' learned in law
And ken the words that break the jaw,
And teinds and processes and a',
Far warse than Greek.
While at the gowff ye' ca' the ba'
Three times a week.

And now and then ye dare confess
Ye drink a social, honest gless.
At Gullan, Islay or Luffness.
Speerits, or rum.
I doubt ye'll hae to Hole wi' less
In Kingdom Come.

For when ye come to Peter's Gate,
He'll say "My man, ye've no that blate
"To think ye'll enter heavenly state
"wi'out a jar.
"My man, ye'll maybe hae to wait
"On something waur.

"Ye had ower guid a time in life,
"Ye lived when honest men were rife,
"Ye werena bothered wi' a wife
"Your easy days
"Were spent across the firth frae Fife.
"A pleasant place.

"We'll hae to give the prior chance
"To folk we led an awfu' dance
"And sent awa' to furrin lands
"'Mong heathen crew
"In India's plains & Afric's sands
"And Timbuctoo.

"On partens now ye'll hae to dine
"Cauld water is your only wine,
"First turnin' to the left, and min'
"The step, my dear."
While I will jink anent ye in
Wi' horrid leer.

I wish ye weel till that dread hour
May health & wealth and friends endure,
And mind me to all friends, be sure,
In toon and clachan,
And I'll subscribe me 'Ever your
                              John Buchan.

J B to Stair Gillon (1903)

May 8, 1903, Governor's Office, Johannesburg.

I

Dear Stair, the best laid schemes o' men
Gang aft agley, as weel ye ken;
We think we're daein' brawly, when
Doon comes the Deevil,
And syne we're roupit but and ben —
It's maist unceevil.

II

Whaur shines the sun on Afric's san'
I hoped that you and me, my man,
Wad traivel in a caravan,
Drove by a neeger,
And kill a gnu wi' our ain han',
Or else a teeger.

III

I hoped to see your Gothic face
And your auld tantit stripit claes
Gang warshin' up the stany braes
Ower rock and scree,
Dod! there had been some cheery days
For you and me!

IV

The *Neeger,*[1] tae — ye ken the man —
Wha to the sons o' Afric's stran'
Instils the history o' their lan',
He was fu' fain
To drink a glass and shake a han'
Wi' you again.

V

Aweel, my dear, it canna be.
For you and Law couldna 'gree.
A kittle limmer she maun be,
A thrawn auld witch
(My langwidge I admit is free)
A donnert bitch!

VI

But when the heather's comin' oot,
And grouse begin to fa' aboot,
And ilka Cockney kills a troot,
Why, Sandy, then
Ye'll see my face wi'oot a doot
At hame again.

VII

And you and me, aiblins, Hugh[2]
Tha Lord kens what we winna do;
We'll make an awfu' rampage through
Baith town and clachan
And so, till then, believe me you —
                    — yrs John Buchan

Stair Gillon includes the following footnotes:
1. John Edgar of Balliol, professor of history at Cape Town.
2. Wyndham.

ॐ   ॐ   ॐ

To a Princess who has Forgotten

'To a Princess who has Forgotten' was Buchan's sixth and last contribution to the *Glasgow University Magazine*. It appeared on 26 January 1898 during Buchan's third year at Oxford.

I would, my dear, that we could go
Far from this dreary mist and snow,
To those lost lands where summer dreams
Lulled all the drowsy silent streams,
That elfin-land beyond recall
Where reigned the Court of Pastoral.

We were two children, you and I,
Unkempt, unwatched, far-wandering, shy,
Trudging from morn with easy load,
While Faery lay adown the road.
Sometimes we found the little town,
On which the castled scarp looked down,
Wherefrom the lonely, wistful child,
The Princess, saw the Goose and smiled; —
Or that strange portal in the hill
By which the white thorn grows at will, —
And she who plucks and decks her breast
Can never more find earthly rest.
Sometimes on sunny summer noon
Our wearied feet got elfin shoon,
And we toiled up the hill so high
We seemed to knock against the sky;
While far among the clouds we heard
The singing of the Snow-white Bird.

Ours were the Gods of elder years —
Or Lady of the Snows and Tears,
Angus the subtle, Conan grey,
And Morag of the Misty Day.
You in such lore were wondrous wise,
My princess of the shining eyes.
Our favour was the Crimson Rose,
Our light the glow worm's lamp, our ways
The Road the King of Errin goes,
And that is to the End of Days.

And now — ah, now our paths have strayed
Far from that happy upland shade;
For we have grown so old, so old,
And I am stiff and you are cold.
Your hair is autumn-brown, your face
Fair with your old inviolate grace;
But now, too clever, you and I,
For simple earth and simple sky,
Must toil and fret and build our plans,
Matching our strength with God's and man's.

So be it, dear. If to achieve,
To stand above the crowd and leave
Old common raptures to the base,
If to press ceaseless in the race
Be happiness, then we may win
To that triumphant Sanhedrin.

But at the last may it not fall
That, from our watch towers scanning all —
Our work, our hope, our labours done,
Our little art beneath the sun,
The petty fame which blinds our eyes,
Our transient philosophies —
There rankle in our hearts a sting?
May it not hap that we shall fling
Our gold aside as earth and dross,
And mourn irrevocable loss?
God knoweth, dear, for at the door
I hear an echo evermore,
Chill as the chill October rain,
"Can ye attain, can ye attain?"

Introduction

John Buchan is now largely remembered as the author of *The Thirty-Nine Steps*, but in the course of a writing life of almost fifty years he wrote over a hundred books which included a series of historical novels, biographies, volumes of short stories and essays, several accounts of real life adventure and even a legal textbook. What few realise is that he was also deeply interested in poetry, publishing a collection of his own poems during the First World War and shortly afterwards compiling an anthology of Scottish poetry.

His love of poetry was inherited from his father, a Free Church minister, who in 1881 published a collection of poetry, *Tweedside Echoes and Moorland Musings*, inspired by the Scottish Borders. The Reverend John Buchan's eldest son would also draw on this countryside for his own work, for though born in Perth in August 1875 and brought up in Glasgow, his childhood holidays were spent with his two sets of grandparents in Peebleshire.

Poetry played a large part in the early lives of Buchan, his two sisters and three brothers. They were brought up on the psalms, on Border ballads and in particular on John Bunyan's allegorical *Pilgrim's Progress* which Buchan learnt by heart. As he grew older he moved on to among others Swinburne and Robert Bridges and through his uncle Willie was introduced to the work of French poets such as Mallarmé and Rimbaud.

His first published verse was a hymn written at the age of eleven for his father's Sunday School but though he continued to write poetry as a teenager he published nothing more until going up to Glasgow University in 1892. There he contributed several poems to the university magazine including 'The Strong Man Armed' and 'To a Princess who was Forgotten'. Three years later he won a scholarship to Brasenose College, Oxford where he resolved to win the Newdigate Poetry Prize, previously won by, among others, Matthew Arnold and Oscar Wilde. On his third attempt Buchan was successful with a poem about the Pilgrim Fathers. This was published by Basil Blackwell and quite widely reviewed. The *Oxford Magazine* praised his use of the heroic couplet and singled out the dedicatory lyric 'To the Adventurous Spirit of the North' as 'a beautiful little piece of work' while the undergraduate paper *Isis*, who detected 'a flavour of Tennyson', thought it 'more readable than the average Newdigate, and — what is of more importance — seems to show greater power of promise.'

In his third year at Oxford Buchan was instrumental in setting up the Horace Society. It met at various colleges where, as he later wrote, members 'supped on nuts and olives and fruits, drank what we made believe was Falernian and read our poetical compositions'. Its members included Maurice Baring, Laurence Binyon, and Hilaire Belloc who wrote 'Sussex Drinking Song' for the Society. Buchan's contributions included 'Ballad of Grey Weather', 'The Gipsy's Song to the Lady Cassilis', 'From the Pentlands looking North and South', 'The Last Song of Oisin' and 'The Soldier of Fortune'. A collection of the members' verses were published in a limited edition of 500 copies in 1901 as *The Book of the Horace Club* by the society's Keeper of the Records, Basil Blackwell.

One of Buchan's first books was *Musa Piscatrix* (1896), an anthology of fishing poems and songs, and even in his novels and essays he includes his own poetry. From his second book *Scholar Gipsies* (1896), a series of essays about Border life, he began his practice of giving a few lines of his own poetry to a character, a device evident in subsequent books such as *John Burnet of Barns* (1898), *A Lost Lady of Old Years* (1899) and *Grey Weather* (1899).

On coming down from Oxford Buchan worked briefly as a barrister in London before going out to South Africa in 1901 for two years to act as private secretary to Lord Milner. Buchan's work was physically and intellectually demanding and he found little time to write anything. Only one poem survives of this period, 'The Semitic Spirit Speaks', a critical look at the sort of self-made Jewish businessman then making millions in South Africa and infiltrating British society. Buchan did not entirely share the ingrained Anti-Semitism of the British Establishment of the period but he certainly despised the rich, rather philistine entrepreneurs, many of them Jewish, who had made fortunes in the South African mines.

South Africa and its legends, however, made a deep impression. 'The Song of the Sea Captain', which has resonances of Coleridge's 'The Rime of the Ancient Mariner', tells the story of a Portuguese sailor who falls in love with the daughter of the great African chieftain Prester John. *Prester John* (1910), a powerful tale about a black man leading a revolt against white settlers, was to be the title of his first commercial success as a novelist.

Prester John was dedicated to a friend from South Africa, Lionel Phillips, and was the second of his books with dedicatory poems to people — the first had been three lines to the Scottish writer Andrew Lang in *Musa Piscatrix*. Other dedications include the lines at the beginning of Buchan's American historical novel *Salute to Adventurers* (1915) to his wife's uncle Sir Reginald Talbot who had been on Sheridan's staff during the American Civil War; the lines to Vernon Watney in *Midwinter* (1923); the poems to his American publisher Ferris Greenslet in *The Courts of the Morning* (1929) and to his brother William, who had recently died, in *The Marquis of Montrose* (1913) and its revision *Montrose* (1928). The latter dedication is one of Buchan's best-known poems. It was included in Archie Wavell's classic anthology *Other Men's Flowers* (1944) and later quoted by Rose Kennedy after the assassination of her son in 1963. Buchan's autobiography had supposedly been one of J.F. Kennedy's favourite books. Indeed several of Buchan's poems are devoted to members of his family. 'In Peebles Churchyard' was written on his father's death and 'A.E.B.' after his youngest brother Alastair was killed at Arras on Easter Monday 1917.

Buchan's reputation as a poet was consolidated with the publication in 1917 of *Poems Scots and English*, a collection of twenty-eight poems half of them in English and half in Scots, which was first published in a limited edition of fifty copies in June 1917 and dedicated to Alastair. Many of his earlier poems are included but a substantial part of the book is devoted to his war poems, which vividly bring alive the courage, companionship, humour and horrors of the Western Front. All of these are written in the Scots vernacular, as if he felt he needed to adopt another more private persona to reflect on what he had seen in his more official position as a war correspondent and official propagandist. Despite the horrors they depict the poems are rather more positive and life-affirming than those of contemporaries such as Siegfried Sassoon, Wilfred Owen, Isaac Rosenberg and Edward Thomas with whom he is sometimes compared. One of the central themes, as with so much in Buchan's writing, is the deeper values and beauty to be found in the Scottish Border countryside that give succour in time of need.

After the Armistice Buchan wrote little in the way of poetry, preferring, now he had four young children, to concentrate on more lucrative creative work such as his novels and biographies. In 1919 he bought Elsfield Manor, just outside Oxford, where he stayed until his appointment as Governor-General of Canada in 1935. However, as his fame as a writer increased an expanded edition of *Poems, Scots and English* was published in 1936. This had eleven new poems, though in fact only five of them had been written since publication of the first edition. The poems in the books published during this period when he was at the height of his fame tend to be dedicatory ones or short ones quoted by characters, with the exception of a long poem, 'Oxford Prologizes', written in 1930 for the Oxford Preservation Trust, and a selection of verse in his last book *The Long Traverse* (1941).

Instead, the years immediately after the First World War were devoted to championing other poets. Throughout the 1920s Buchan edited a series of poetry anthologies for the publisher Thomas Nelson ranging from Robert Browning to Dante Gabriel Rossetti and he developed a particular interest in Scottish writing. In 1915 he had written a preface to Violet Jacob's *Songs of Angus* and in 1931 edited *The Poetry of Neil Munro* for *Blackwood's*. During these fifteen years between moving to Oxford and leaving for Canada, Buchan became friendly with Christopher Murray Grieve, better known as the poet Hugh McDiarmid. The two greatly admired each other's work. Grieve, who was to later describe Buchan as 'Dean of the Faculty of Contemporary Scottish Letters', dedicated his *Annals of the Five Senses* to Buchan and in 1925 Buchan wrote the introduction to Grieve's *Sangschaw*.

In 1920 Grieve had invited Buchan to be the first of eleven Scottish poets to be included in *Northern Numbers*, described by the publishers T.N. Foulis as 'being representative selections from certain living Scottish poets'. Three Buchan poems were included — 'Fratri Dilectissimo', 'Fisher Jamie' and 'From the Pentlands Looking North and South'. The following year a second series was produced with Lewis Spence joining seven of the original eleven. Again Buchan was chosen to lead the book, this time with 'The Gipsy's Song to the Lady Cassilis', 'The Wise Years' and 'Wood Magic'.

Northern Numbers had been the first attempt to collect and assess the poetry produced by the burgeoning Scottish Literary Renaissance. Buchan realized the need for a more comprehensive anthology drawing on Scotland's rich poetical past if the renaissance was to be sustained. In 1924 he edited for Nelson *The Northern Muse: an Anthology of Scots Vernacular Poetry*. He stressed in the introduction that it was very much a personal selection but both the introduction and the widely praised commentary of notes at the end showed him to have read and thought deeply about the subject. The two hundred and forty-five poems were divided not chronologically but thematically into eighteen subject areas such as 'Youth and Spring', '*Plaisir D'Armour*', 'Sport', 'Death' and 'Divine Philosophy'. There were the obvious inclusions such as William Dunbar, Robert Burns, Allan Ramsay, Sir Walter Scott, Robert Fergusson and R.L. Stevenson but he also introduced younger or lesser-known poets including Grieve and a young barrister, later Speaker of the House of Commons, W.S. Morrison. He also included three of his own poems — 'On Leave', 'Fisher Jamie' and 'The Fishers' from the Theocritus in Scots translation.

The Northern Muse received good and extensive review coverage, particularly in the *Spectator* from his former editor there St Loe Strachey, and an Oxford neighbour Robert Graves who, writing in *The Nation & Athenaeum*, thought Buchan had 'achieved the distinction of being the first man to make a comprehensive anthology of Scottish and Northern English poetry which Southerns can read with real pleasure'. Graves added: 'The notes at the end are copious and scholarly beyond suspicion, and there is a fine introduction, but the most remarkable feat of editorship has been in keeping *The Northern Muse* within the decent bounds of sentiment.' The most cherished praise came from Grieve who felt the book stood 'in relation to Scots poetry as Palgrave's *Golden Treasury* to English . . . a definitive book, supplying a long-felt want in a fashion that seems likely to give such an impetus to Scottish poetry that it will stand as a landmark in our literary history.'

Throughout the inter-war period Buchan was widely anthologised, particularly in collections of Scottish poetry where he appeared alongside Marion Angus, George Douglas Brown, Violet Jacob, Neil Munro, Eric Linklater, Hugh McDiarmid, Edwin Muir and Lewis Spence as well as Robert Burns, James Hogg, Allan Ramsay and R.L. Stevenson. Among the anthologies of the period to include Buchan poems were *A St Andrews Treasury of Scottish Verse* (1920), *A Book of Scots* (1925), *A Book of Twentieth Century Verse* (1925), *A Scots Garland* (1931), *A Book of Twentieth Century Scots Verse* (1932), *The Scots Book* (1935) and *The Scots Weekend* (1936).

Buchan's poetry, like his books, is marked by a variety of influences based on his wide reading. His upbringing as a child of the Scottish manse can be seen in 'Midian's Evil Day', 'Babylon' and 'The Shorter Catechism'. His Classical education is evident in poems such as 'An Echo of Meleager', 'Atta's Song' and the free translations of the Greek pastoral poet Theocritus's poems into Scots. Several of his poems are even written in Latin, most notably the ode to Alison Westwater in *The House of the Four Winds* (1935). His love of French poetry is reflected by several poems written in French, most notably in his countryhouse discussion novel about imperialism *A Lodge in the Wilderness* (1906) and his paraphrase of Victor Hugo's 'Guitaure' as 'Jock's Song' (1916).

There are traces of Yeats in 'Ballad for Grey Weather', Kipling in 'Plain Folk' and 'Babylon' and Browning in 'The Wise Years'. The influence of Sir Walter Scott, R.L. Stevenson, Keats, Matthew Arnold, William Morris, Robert Bridges and Lord Tennyson is also evident throughout his work. Indeed one of the criticisms directed against Buchan's early poetry is that it is too derivative, has little to say and draws too heavily on the then cult of the pastoral. He only seems to have found his own voice when he wrote in the Scots vernacular.

It is perhaps appropriate then that he should be remembered, as he was by his contemporaries, as primarily a Scots poet. A large number of his poems celebrate the Scottish, and in particular Border, countryside such as the much anthologised 'The South Countrie' and many of them express an exile's longing for Scotland such as 'Avignon'. One of Buchan's greatest skills as a writer was his ability to evoke the sounds, smell and sights of the countryside, a skill demonstrated in his novels, short stories and biographies but most potently displayed in his poetry.

Buchan is often accused of snobbery, of being more interested in the successful and talented than in the ordinary working man. This may be true of some of the 'shockers', but is certainly not true of either the historical novels or the poetry. Apart from a few dedicatory poems to family or friends Buchan's poetry celebrates the lives and aspirations of ordinary people, most of them Scottish, whether it is 'Plain Folk' or 'Fisher Jamie', a lament for a Border lad killed in the war never happier than with his fishing rod. This ability to convey the commonplaces of daily life was combined with a strong mystic sense and vivid historical imagination. This is reflected in several of his novels, such as *The Dancing Floor* (1926) and *Witch Wood* (1927), and in poems such as 'Wood Magic' written in 1910 after an episode, described in his memoirs, of encountering a spirit in a Bavarian forest.

His highly developed ear for language, demonstrated by the cadences of his prose and his ability to write convincing dialogue, meant he was also able to write good pastiche. This gift was more obviously apparent as an undergraduate in his poetic collaborations with Raymond Asquith, but there are signs of it later in life such as his 1913 satirical poem (with apologies to Matthew Arnold) about contemporary politics *'Thyrsis de nos jours'* and his reworking in 1937 of 'O Mistress Mine' as it might have been revised for a Hollywood film. A number of unpublished poems survive which seem to have been privately circulated, principally during the First World War, among friends. They include a twelve-page dramatic burlesque 'The Argonauts at Delphi' about Gerard Craig-Sellar and Alec Maitland, a poem on Lady Leconfield 'A Doleful Ballad of a Certain Noble Lady' and a burlesque on Burns 'Holy Johnie's Prayer'. Other poems, bound in the two volume collection originally in the possession of Buchan's daughter Alice, include poems by Max Beerbohm, Hilaire Belloc, Ronald Knox, Henry Newbolt, Raymond Asquith, Julian Grenfell, Osbert Sitwell and Charles Masterman.

Given that he was an essentially private man and rarely revealed his inner thoughts in his writing Buchan's poetry gives perhaps the clearest indication of his true feelings. It truly comes alive when he is writing about an individual or has been deeply affected by a particular event. This may be why many recent critics think his best poetry was written in Scots and that his war poetry stands out as his finest achievement. It was not a view shared by the *TLS* in their review of *Poems, Scots and English* on its first publication:

> Every one reading Mr Buchan's Scottish poems will be struck by the contrast between those about the war and those of the older world. It is not merely that some of the poems are peaceful; it is more than that . . . They belong to any time or no time; they are contemporary with all Scottish verse of the school of Ramsay and Burns; they admit you to the pastoral eternity of that old world which lies at the back of the hills. The war poems, good as they are, have not this sort of magic quality . . .

Perhaps because it was such a private part of him Buchan was modest about his poetry and does not even mention it in his memoirs. As a result it has been ignored by many commentators since his death. Janet Adam Smith in her 1965 biography makes a few passing comments about individual poems but does not even refer to *Poems, Scots and English* while William Buchan in his 1982 memoir of his father simply mentions it as one of his father's books. Given, also, that Buchan wrote less than fifty full-length poems there is a limited body of work to study, which may have put off some critics. However in his own lifetime Buchan made the most of his poetry and had no qualms about using his poems time and time again. The introductory lines to his 1899 Newdigate Prize Poem appear in *The Long Traverse* written some forty years later, while verse first found in *Grey Weather* (1899) is only slightly transposed in *Witch Wood* (1927). His poem 'From the Pentlands Looking North and South' was written originally for the Horace Club at Oxford but then included in his volume of short stories *The Moon Endureth* (1912), as a contribution to the first series of *Northern Numbers* in 1920 and finally added to Susan Buchan's anthology of her husband's work *The Clearing House* in 1946. Buchan's contribution to Scottish literature recognised in his own day is finally being appreciated again now. Many of the themes to be found in his books — the redemptive power of nature, the conflict between self and state, the frontier between romance and realism — are also to be found in his poems and therefore are attracting scholars interested in his prose. Few tributes on his death in February 1940 mentioned his poetry. It is for his 'shockers' and his role as a public servant that Buchan will be rightly remembered but his poetry should not as a result be dismissed. Some of it is very powerful indeed and it sheds a light on the more private, reflective man that is rarely glimpsed in the pictures taken by Karsh or the prose of *The Thirty Nine Steps*.

A New Year's Hymn   *(1887)*

This is the first published verse by John Buchan, and it was written under the name of 'A Scholar' for the Pathhead Free Church Sabbath School. It is now in the John Buchan Centre at Broughton.

To Thee, Our God and Friend,
　　We raise our hymn to-day;
Oh, guard and guide us from above
　　Along life's troubled way.

A year has passed away,
　　Another has begun;
Oh, keep us safely by Thy power,
　　Until life's race is run.

Our hope is stayed in Thee,
　　No other friend so near;
Thou art a very present help
　　To such as do Thee fear.

Oh, make us, Lord, to walk
　　Within the narrow way;
Give unto us Thy saving grace,
　　That we may never stray.

The mercies, Lord, are great
　　Which Thou to us hast given;
They meet us at each turn in life,
　　To lead us on to heaven.

Like to the morning mist,
　　Earth's glory soon shall die;
Oh, lead us onward till we reach
　　Our happy home on high.

　　　　　　　　By a Scholar

8

Early Poems 1892 to 1895

The following hand-written poems were discovered within a file of 'unpublished writings' in the archives of Queen's University, Kingston. They are authenticated by an accompanying letter, addressed to John Buchan, from the Reverend Charles H. Dick, dated 30 July 1938.

The relevant extract from the letter reads:

> I was rumaging through some old collections of papers the other day and came upon the enclosed *juvenilia*, which should be in your hands. The gaps in the paging were designed, I believe, to give space for some of my early poetical works. [Rev. Dick is referring to the gaps in the sequence of roman numerals which in this work appear to the left of some of the poem titles in this section, and were the page numbers in the original work.] It has been quite thrilling to read again those from your pen and to recall the places where some of them were written!

Unfortunately the poems are undated, though it is suspected they were written while John Buchan and Charles Dick were at Glasgow University; they certainly traipsed the hills together during those years (1892 to 1895).

In *Memory Hold the Door* (1940) Buchan writes:

> . . . and my earliest poetic effort was not lyrical but epic, the first canto of a poem on Hell.

Could it be that [XXXIX] entitled 'The Norus' is that very poem?

It is also interesting to note the poem entitled 'On a Portrait of the Hon. Mrs Graham by Gainsborough' [XVIII]. When allocated his room at Oxford in October 1895 it contained a painting of that very same lady.

The Piper

I

Where has the Piper gone to-day?
    Does he still linger at our sides?
Or does he sojourn far away
    In other lands by other tides?
Forsooth I think he is not far,
    In mart and lane and crowded street:
Amid the traffic's roar and jar
    We hear the tripping of his feet.

II

He passes through the stately hall
    Where strong-browed sage in council sits,
At junketing and carnival
    Amid the throng his shadow flits.
He plays amid the cloisters dim,
    To men of woe and men of laughter,
And whether it be catch or hymn
    They lightly rise and follow after.

III

He plays to lad, he plays to lass,
    To youth, to those whose years are riper,
To maiden smirking at the glass,
    This whimsical and curious Piper.
To weary men at desk or loom
    He pipes of field and bowery hollow.
They bid adieu to dusty room,
    And set them out and onward follow.

IV

And to poor poets he has played,
    And unto them his note is kind;
For they like him have somewhat strayed;
    They are according to his mind.
He leads them out by dale and hill,
    Green country lane and flower-clad mead in,
To where they wander at their will
    And find a new and better Eden.

To some he pipes a noble tune
      Of lordlier lands across the sea,
Of coral coast and still lagoon,
      Of heath and hill and desert free.
And as they rise with dauntless soul
      And haste to do his high behest,
And riding as the seasons roll
      They proudly pass from East to West.

VI

To all at last the Piper plays
      With eldrich guise and mournful song;
To men he brings the end of days
      And they must haste and march along.
To some his tune is dim and sad,
      To others fraught with happy wonder.
To maid and hag, to sage and lad
      He pipes his tune and plays them under.

VII

So if you hear at even tide
      Or when the morn is freshly risen,
By woodland path or riverside
      Or in the city's dismal prison,
A sound so quaint and queer and high,
      A mingling strange of grief and laughter,
Then know the Piper passes by,
      So get you out and follow after.

I

The Spring was bright and shining as a flower;
  More green the grass than any green before.
The woodlands dripping with the fallen shower
  Shone like great jewels; and, when as of yore
  The year had passed the Summer's dusky door,
Strange colours richer than the Orient dyes
  Dwelt in the tulips and the roses' store,
And weird lights passed at even and sunrise
O'er the translucent blue of the fair Summer skies.

II

The Autumn came; the yellow-headed stalks
  Bent in the wheatlands with their weight of corn;
The apples hanging o'er the orchard walks,
  The peaches rosy with the flush of morn,
The russet pears, the wild-fruits on the thorn,
  Were larger, riper, than in elder years;
The great red berries which the rose adorn,
  And the soft apricot the south-wall rears
Shone like a young maid's face when her true love appears.

III

Yet when the harvest sheaves were gathered in,
  And when men sought to crush the golden grain,
No need was there for flail or threshing din,
  The husk was empty; nought did there remain.
Then loud the grieving o'er the fruitful plain,
  For every fruit so fresh and fair of hue
But dust and ashes did within contain;
  Nor any food was found the whole world through,
Then fell on every man harsh pain and bitter rue.

Meantime strange sounds were borne along the air,
    Now of men singing, now the cry of woe,
Now as when some old lion from his lair
    Sends his last roar across the forest low.
    And evermore the sorrow seemed to grow;
Hard voices and black forms the skies affright;
    While in the cities low winds to and fro
Made fearful moaning eke by day and night,
And like lost faces passed dim shapes and phantoms white.

V

The dank leaves dripped and rotted on the trees,
    And glowed in gaunt effulgence of decay,
Nor shaken were the boughs with pleasant breeze,
    But silent still and deathly quiet alway.
In the lush grass, made with loathsome spray,
    Thick fungus growths made foul the laden air.
All woodland flowers had fled in dire dismay;
    Here bloomed no heath nor gold-rod standing fair,
But dull green creepers twined and coiled like dead men's hair.

VI

And oft at even ere the sun was set,
    And men were weary with the awesome day,
The world grew black though darkness was not yet,
    And, as the sun went down the western way,
Athwart the dim expanse of endless gray
    Huge clouds of crimson, like a coronal,
And strange, bright colours hung in close array;
    Then all men shuddered at the last year's fall,
And waited sick at heart till came the end of all.

An Old Flower Garden

I

When the fairy-footed Spring,
    Rising like a maiden,
Cometh swift on airy wing,
    With the bounties laden;
When her dainty lips have kissed
    Darkness from the hollow —
Clothed in mist of amethyst —
    Rise and let me follow.

II

In my garden by the heath,
    Near the moorlands hilly,
Where from out her grassy sheath
    Riseth up the lily,
By the green, old, border ring,
    'Neath the elm-trees shady,
Let us sing unto the Spring,
    "Welcome thou, my Lady."

III

Sparrows chatter in the eaves;
    Linnets sing in hedges;
Blackbirds pipe among the leaves,
    Warblers in the sedges.
Snowdrop shy and crocus bright
    Glimmer in the border.
Daffodillies stand upright,
    Gay in gallant order.

IV

Mazed like pale Persephone
    'Mid Sicilian bowers,
Droops the white anemone
    'Mong the ruddy flowers.
Clouds of blossom, pink and white,
    Iris-stately warden —
Springtide flowers, a goodly sight,
    In my shadowed garden.

14

An Evening by the Sea

The day is done; the tired land looks for night
(Robert Bridges)

I

Some men love the dawning
    When the morn comes out of the sea;
And some the yellow noontide
    When the sun shines merrily.
But give me rather the evening
    In the little, grey, Northern town,
When over the firth and the harbour
    The sun goes down.

II

The white clouds drift to the Southward
    Like wings of an angel quire.
The long-ribbed hills to the Westward
    Glow like a furnace fire;
And down on the shimmering sea-plain,
    That jewelled mirror of light,
Crimson and carmine and purple,
    The hues of the night.

III

The quaint red roofs of the hamlet,
    The sea-grey harbour wall,
The shingle, pebbled and shell-strown,
    The dark cliffs, jagged and tall,
The fishermen's bronzed brown faces,
    The fair fisher lass by their side
Are bathed in the mellow sunlight
    Of the golden eventide.

IV

And often I dream that yonder,
    Beyond the red sea haze,

15

Is that wonderful El Dorado
  Men sung of in former days;
Where is heard the sound of dead voices,
  And many a fair face greets,
And boys and girls are singing
  And playing in the streets.

The Happy Valley

I

I know a vale among the long blue hills
Which cast their shadows o'er the waves of Clyde.
From the brown slopes where no man ever tills
Its golden pastures stretch on either side
The river running wide,
By lichened stone and willowy copses going,
Fed by the waters of a thousand rills
From the high rocks and mountain lakelets flowing.

II

At noon the shadows sleep upon the grass,
Where the slim harebell and pale woodruff grow.
Stray sungleams creep among the blossoming mass
Of hawthorns past and wild rose trailing low;
While alway to and fro
Dart swift-winged swallows from the South lands coming,
And honey-laden bees the waters pass,
And make the dead air living with their humming.

III

By the deep pool whereto the river glides
Grow irises and mint and lilies rare,
And sometimes leaping in the shining tides
The trout, red-speckled, riseth to the air;
And o'er the margin fair
Hang hazels and green birks the current lining,
Busking in shadow all the flower-clad sides
With woodbines, ivy and sweet-briars intwining.

IV

O'er the gray rocks the white-flowered brambles climb,
And lady-ferns their dainty fronds upraise.
The breeze is fragrant with the scent of thyme
Borne downward from the healthy mountain ways;
And in the Summer days

The eglantines their delicate odours mingle
With the sleep-soothing fragrance of the lime
Which shades the stream in every dell and dingle.

V

Sometimes an angler, climbing the cascade
O'er which the river seeks the distant plains,
Makes of the roots and heath and escalade
And wins the vale, wherein he straightway gains
Much fish for all his pains;
But on returning he is straight forgetting
The teeming river and the pleasant glade,
Remembering but the sorrows it besetting.

VI

Sometimes a shepherd, seeking his strayed flocks,
Wanders by chance into this happy land,
And, wearied with the mountains and the rocks,
Lies down and slumbers by the river strand;
And dreams of golden sand,
And, waking, finds his charge about him lowing,
And drives them home, while memory ever mocks,
For of the place and path he is unknowing.

[XIV]   *Plato*

I picture thee as one with high
Broad brow and gaze divinely keen,
With a great gravity of eye,
And wondrous quietude of mien,

With kindly tone and pleasant speech,
Tired dusty feet and threadbare gown,
And face sun-browned as autumn beech
With wandering through the Attic town.

18

[XV]   *Marcus Aurelius*

O thou my Soul, thou lord of many mansions,
Who art my life, and all earth's joy to me,
Haste with swift wing from forth thy dim expansions;
Make thou me free.

Grant me this gift, I pray thee, O my master,
For which I yearn as seeker for the sought,
More rare than gold, more fair than alabaster, —
One perfect thought,

Strong with the strength of masterful endeavour,
Rich with exceeding wealth divinely given,
And fair as waters where the pale stars quiver,
And high as Heaven.

[XVI]   *Hereafter*

We know not now, but we shall know
Hereafter, in a clear-day,
The things untold, the mystic way
Which God hath walked from long ago;

The secrets of the silent skies,
The love, the immemorial strength;
Then shall we know the breadth, the length,
The truth of the philosophies.

From men long kept shall open be
The hidden things of death and birth,
The wonders of the glad, green earth,
The mysteries of the old, gray sea.

And life's long tale of good and ill,
The fancies which the poets sing;

19

Why flutes the mavis in the Spring,
How pipes the linnet on the hill.

But chief for thee, dear heart, I long,
Dear heart, long lost, again to hear
Thy sweet voice mellow in mine ear,
Like echo of an ancient song.

[XVIII]   *On a Portrait of the Hon. Mrs Graham by Gainsborough*

Dear dead women — with such hair too
(Browning)

Tall and stately there thou standest, looking as in days of old,
When the painter on his canvas drew those glowing locks of
        gold,

Dressed in quaintest, richest fashion, in the style of long ago,
With thy flounces of white satin and thy lace of Iacotot.

Beautiful thou art and haughty, with a royal head and eye,
Standing by the pillared sailing, 'neath a grey and dusky sky.

All around are woodlands shady. Shadow dark thy beauty
        frames;
Thou thyself the fairest lady in an age of noble dames.

Well we know thy mournful story, of the passing of thy bloom,
How thy husband's heart and pleasures lay beside thee in the
        tomb;

How he mourned in sorest sorrow, pacing ever through the hall,
And in grief for thee his lost love turned thy picture to the wall.

How he raised his clan, and, eager, sought the battle's hottest
        fray,
Stoutly warred, and at Barossa won the honour of the day.

20

Years have gone and they have found thee, scarcely dimmed by
 dust and time,
Bright and radiant still, fair-coloured, glorying in thy beauty's
 prime.

Men and women, all have perished; gone the painter, too,
 forsooth;
But his handiwork, thy picture, liveth in immortal youth.

Still thou standest, haughty, stately, on thy cheek a rosy glow,
With thy flounces of white satin and thy lace of Iacotot.

John Buchan added a footnote to this Poem, it reads:

> This picture had been walled up for many years, and has only comparatively recently been discovered. On the death of his wife, her husband, unable to endure his grief at home, raised a force and went to the war in Spain, where he so distinguished himself that he won the name of the 'Hero of Barossa'.

[XX]   *The Dead Scholar*
                        (Callimachus)

                        Anth. Pal VII. 80.

 One told me, Heraclitus, of thy fate;
 I wept, and minded me how oft we twain
 Had held high converse till the day was late,
 And the broad sun was setting with his train.

 And thou art ashes long and long ago,
 O Halicarnian; but thy deathless band
 Of nightingales shall live for evermore.
 No Death can lay on them his plundering hand.

21

[XXI]

The Orchard
(Anyte)

Anth. Pal. IX. 314.

I, Hermes, stand by the windy ways, by the orchard, nigh
The gray shore of the sea.
Rest I give to the wearied man, to the passer-by,
And water cold and free.

[XXII]

Erinna
(Leonidas of Tarentum)
Anth. Pal. VII. 13.

The maid Erinna, child among the old,
The bee who sucked from flowers the Muse's breath,
Death snatched for marriage, and the maiden bold
Spake wisely, "Thou art curious, O Death."

[XXVI]

Spring and Death
'Solvitur aeris heimo' etc.
(Hor.)

The Spring returns, the West Winds blow;
Across the foam the vessels go;
No more the cattle seek the byre;
The farmer leaves his winter fire;
The hoar frost rimes the field with snow.

Around thy brow the myrtle throw,
For Graces trip it to and fro,
And Cytherea leads her choir,
When Spring returns.

22

Death comes alike to high and low;
Our hopes are riven ere we know.
To-day beholds thee strike the lyre,
Another morn may see the pyre.
Ah! Never in the realms below
                    Will Spring return.

Trioleto

This poem is not numbered and the title has been crossed out.

I

I quite agree with you, my friend
'Tis but an idle triolet;
Of making which there is no end;
I quite agree with you, my friend,
'Tis wrong my time to verse to lend
Which every rule doth violate.
I quite agree with you, my friend,
'Tis but an idle triolet.

II

The rain is over and gone,
The mist has left the hill;
Bright the sun hath shone,
The rain is over and gone;
But put your greatcoat on;
The evening air is chill.
The rain is over and gone,
The mist hath left the hill.

III

If fairy tunes were fairy gold;
Then, ah, how rich we bards would be;
For then by every wood and wold,
If fairy tunes were fairy gold,

We'd gather treasures manifold.
A happy time for you and me!
If fairy tunes were fairy gold,
Then, ah! how rich we bards would be.

[XXIX]   *In Glen Eaisdale*

In the September days' late afternoon
The skies above are blue and cold and still;
The glen is sleeping with its heath and hill;
In the black pinewoods low the pigeons croon.

Ah would that man could learn the heavenly tune
Of silence and the peace that quiet begets,
And in the market-place of thousand frets
Read the quaint writ of this forgotten rune.

For soon we pass with all our work undone,
Our silver and our houses are as nought;
Our raiment and apparel which we wrought

With toil and trouble ere our sands were run,
But still the breeze with honey-scents is fraught,
And o'er the midmost mountain shines the sun.

[XXX]   *A Moorland Ballade*

Up on the hills when the wind is free,
And the strong air glows like a draught of wine,
And the royal sun glints merrily
Over the heather and woods of pine,
I envy thee not the woodlands thine,
Thy sleepy rivers and meadows gay;

Keep thy roses and eglantine,
But give, oh give me the moorlands gray.

Then doth the heart grow high with glee
When the hill bees hum in the blithe sunshine.
Cares of the past and the things to be
Pass like ships on the swift-waved brine.
Some men love the olive and vine,
Some the plains and the dusty way,
Some the fields of the large-eyed kine,
But give, oh give me the moorlands gray.

Fair are the brackens and tenderly
Scents of thyme and heather combine;
Fairer far than the clover lea,
Ivies over the boulders twine.
Here alone in the hills divine,
Care and weariness pass away;
Grant me this boon, Ye Muses Nine,
Give, oh give me the moorlands gray.

Lands and houses and raiment fine,
What are they but a vain display?
Gladly I all to others resign,
But give, oh give me the moorlands gray.

[XXXII]   *On a Certain Affected Obscurity of Style*

'They shoot but calm words folded up in smoke To make a faithless error in your ears.'
(King John)

Some men there are who love not simple speech,
But needs must wrap their truth in clouds of dust,
Weakening the terror of their strong sword's thrust
With mail of nothingness; for still they reach

25

And blindly aim and toil and fight and teach,
With half their work undone, for half doth seem
But as the fitful phasing of a dream
Or the light wave-foam on a sanded beach.

For better sure the white, pellucid page
Of courtly Sidney, or the majestic calm
Of the sweet dreamer, or the noble rage

Of Milton and the quaint-turned phrase of Lamb;
Or the strong words clear borne across the age
From the wise mouth of great-browed Verulam.

[XXXIII]   *Autumn*

O daughter of the fading gold,
        Crowned with sere leaves and berries red,
Thou comest when the year is old.

Let all thy sober charms be told,
        Thy stately form, thy wreathéd head,
O daughter of the fading gold.

Red russet robes thy breasts enfold,
        By thee the harvest feast is spread;
Thou comest when the year is old.

Thine are the fruits in field and wold,
        In orchard close and garden bed,
O daughter of the fading gold.

The woods grow bare; the nights are cold;
        The skies are dark; the flowers are dead,
Thou comest when the year is old.

But still to thee let hymns be rolled,
        And white steers to the altar led.

O daughter of the fading gold,
Thou comest when the year is old.

ॐ ॐ ॐ

An Autumn Picture

As here I sit this languid Autumn day,
Before me stretch great shores of sunset leaves,
Crowning the gaunt boughs ere the wind bereaves
The woods of these, the lingering leaves of May.

Crimson and golden in a death display
Bright flare the blossoms of the falling year.
Now gone the green of beech, and cold and sere
The yielding hazel. All the skies are gray.

High from the wild woods stretch the upland spaces,
Brown is the bent and cumbered with dead bloom;
No cheerful song of lark the moorland thrills;

But dim and distant gleam the mountain places,
And, hovering half in daylight and in gloom,
The clear October shadows fold the hills.

ॐ ॐ ॐ

[XXXVIII] **The Snow Queen**

I saw the Snow Queen in her chariot fare,
Drawn by twin steeds, clean-limbed and vigorous.
Full well she drove, most swift and valorous
Through the gray storm-clouds and the rustling air.

All robed in furs of ermine and of vair,
Whence shone the blossom of her starlike face,
Crowned with the wreathing of her golden grace,
The weird, unutterable beauty of her hair.

27

And well I know that ill befalls the wight
Who seeks her love and with her followeth;
For she with her fell witchery shall him smite,

And freeze his heart's blood with her frosty breath.
For, though her beauty be most rare and bright,
Her kiss is mortal as the embrace of Death.

[XXXIX]   *The Norus*

'A fair hall stands under the ash by the spring, and out of it came three maidens, Norus,
named *Has-been*, *Being*, *Will-be*, who guide the lives of men.'

The Prose Edda

I saw the fair hall by the holy well,
Hard by the shadow of the sacred tree
Yggdrasil, where the worm gnaws endlessly,
And whose one root extendeth down to Hell;

Wherein the maids, men call the Norus, do dwell,
Who draw the living water day by day,
And strew the ash-boughs with the healing clay,
Who shape the lives of man and damosel.

The elder Urd, sat high and dark and old,
With guise of one whose day is finishéd;
In midst Verdandi, chill and wintry cold,

Clear-faced as ice and girt with death and dread;
While skuld apart, though all in duck enfold,
Had a dim aureole circling o'er her head.

Death

Why should a brave man fear the warrior Death,
Who cometh girt as strong man for the fray,
O'er the hilltops when the skies are gray,
Ere the fair sunrise comes, he hasteneth.

And all green things are withered at his breath.
He with clear voice and welcome words doth say,
'Thy time hath come, rise, let us haste away',
And o'er the mountains back he followeth.

While men of sinking faith and courage small
He guides by dismal alley and hard way,
By dark woodpath where never sunbeams fall,

Men of stout heart, to whom the world is fair,
With no sick soul nor any weary day,
Pass o'er the mountains in the cool, bright air.

[XLII]   *Kyrielle*

Down in the valley the sun is bright;
Hollows glow in the Autumn light;
But ever we dream of a brighter day
Over the Hills and faraway.

Fair are the lawns and woodlands deep,
Pastures sunk in a Summers sleep;
But we know of happier sights than they
Over the Hills and faraway.

Skies with never an angry cloud,
Woods where never the wind pipes loud,
Meadows peopled by faun and fay
Over the Hills and faraway.

And thus from Dawning unto Dark,
From the evensong to the early lark,
Siren whisperings ever say
Over the Hills and faraway.

ॐ ॐ ॐ

The remaining poems in this collection of early works are not numbered

Giordano Bruno

Oh, to have lived in thy triumphant time,
When 'mid the gloom and ruin of outworn creed,
And snarling churchmen and the felon breed
Of monks apostate, and the lust of crime,

Thou grandly held'st thy head erect, sublime;
With some few brothers sought a better home,
And dashed the gauntlet in the face of Rome,
And died ere yet the passing of thy prime.

Oh, that with thee I had had the strength to stand,
Serene, unconquerable, still reaching higher,
With some fair vision of a mystic land
Before mine eyes to which I should aspire;
And, o'er the shouting of the rabble band
Follow to freedom, even through the fire.

ॐ ॐ ॐ

The Song of all Seasons

Blue the sky and gray the hill,
Pan is singing, Pan is playing,
Up and down the vale at will
Lad and lasses go a-maying.
Shy cuckoo and throstle gay
By the bank and brake are winging,

All the world has gone to play,
Pan is piping, Pan is singing.

Waters sleep and woods are green,
Pan is singing, Pan is playing,
Bud and leaf and bloom between
List Sir Poet lackadaying.
Morning gold and evening red,
Summer at our feet is flinging
Who is not a-wander led?
Pan is piping, Pan is singing.

Nuts a-tremble in the wood,
Pan is singing, Pan is playing,
In the mountain solitude
Heath and heather fair arraying;
Golden sheaf and russet fruit
Men into their stores are bringing,
Woods are silent, birds are mute
Pan is piping, Pan is singing.

Still the world beneath the snow,
Pan is singing, Pan is playing,
By the wood does winter go
On the streams his sceptre laying;
Though the earth be chill and cold,
Though no bard his lyre is stringing,
Still across the wintry wold
Pan is piping, Pan is singing.

The Ballad of Gideon Scott

Oh, ye may ride by the Annan side,
    Up the dale and down;
South ye may go to the Solway Flow,
    And North to Moffat town.

But fare not near, if the ford ye fear,
    And the pains of death ye dread;
Yea, ride as well to the gate of Hell
    As the moors of Erickstanehead.

Gideon Scott was a reiver bold,
    And fray was his delight;
No man could dare on the Border fair
    To meet with him in fight.
His arm was strong as the young yew tree,
    His heart as the young stag's thigh;
His eye saw far as the Kite's in war,
    When the wounded foemen die.

It fell upon the Martinmas tide,
    When the skies are gray and cold,
When the night falls black and the winds are out
    And the sheep are in the fold,
That the tidings came from Moffatdale
    That the English men were strong
To harry and hunt and carry and lift
    And work their neighbours wrong.

Then up and out spake Gideon Scott
    And an angry man was he,
"May blight and curse fall on my house
    And sorrow come upon me,
If Hall and Reid from over the Tweed
    Shall hunt and harry here,
While a Scottish man may mount a steed
    Or his arm may lift a spear."

Now he has saddled his good gray horse,
    And he has ridden away.
The night was black as the mouth of a pit,
    And wild as the Judgment Day;
And he has ridden by moor and bent,
    Field and castle and tree,
For his mind was high and his heart was wroth
    And an angry man was he.

He rode by the bent and he rode by the stream,
        Many a mile and far
By bank and lea and ford and tree,
        Bield and tussock and scaur;
But he scarce had won to the Half-way Stane,
        Scarce to the Birkit Mound,
When his horse fell lame i' the howe of a burn,
        And sank upon the ground.

Then Gideon Scott he leapt to his feet
        And a desp'rate man was he.
He swore by devil, he swore by saint,
        He swore by the Holy Three.
And then he swore an awesome oath,
        As never a man before;
"My soul I'll sell to the Lord of Hell
        For a horse to carry me o'er."

Scarce the word had left his mouth
        And gone to the ear of God,
When he was aware of a coal-black mare,
        Stood pawing on the sod.
Black she stood from neck to hoof,
        Black from tail to mane;
Her eyes were fire and her heart was ire,
        And she sniffed across the plain.

Never a word he spake but quick
        He bitted and saddled the black,
He strapped the girth and buckled the belt
        And leapt upon her back.
And he's away on the awesome mare
        By an awesome purchase bought;
"But I care not a span for beast or man
        Or fiend", quo' Gideon Scott.

The gray had ridden like flying cloud,
        But the black like a hag by night;
The gray had leapt like the young roe-deer,
        But the black like a fiend in flight.

By bank and lea, by ford and tree,
            Bield and tussock and scar,
By bent and moor by field and stream,
            Many a mile and far.

And they have come to the Annan Water,
            And it ran high and red.
Never a man might ford it safe,
            Nor horse i' the Border bred.
But the mare has flown like a swallow in Spring,
            Clear from bank to brae.
There was never such leap in the world before,
            Nor has been to this day.

Now he has come to Moffatdale,
            And a glow is in the sky
Of blazing thatch and burning stack,
            And the fiery splinters fly.
He has heard the cry of wounded men,
            The roar of a conquering foe;
And he bites his lip and spurs his steed
            And nerves him for a blow.

Like the Winter rain across the plain
            In hurrying gust they ride;
Like a bolt from God they scour the sod,
            And never a moment bide.
They scatter through crowds of fighting men,
            Din and clatter and blaze;
And they are out on the bent again,
            And off on the mountain ways.

And strange I ween must the sight have been
            To Southron and to Scot,
A coal-black horse and an angry man
            Past like a musket-shot.
And little they recked of fight and fray,
            Cattle and plunder share;
But each man fell on his bended knee
            And strove to mutter a prayer.

A fearful man was Gideon Scott,
      With terror was he ta'en;
And he strove to leap from the flying mare,
      But ever he strove in vain.
For swifter still the black mare flew,
      And stranger was the way,
And the night grew black as the mouth of a pit,
      And wild as the Judgment Day.

Now they have passed by the Wildshaw Burn,
      And o'er by the Mirkshaw Head;
The water splashed and the marsh-fire flashed
      At the sound of the horse's tread.
As a Winter stream or an angry cloud
      They fled by the gray Hartfell,
By tussock and tree, by ridge and lea,
      Stream and water and well.

They rode by the rushing Annan stream
      Red from fray to bank,
And twice the mare has swum across
      And never her shoulders sank.
They scoured the glen from mouth to end
      By hill and water and way,
To the place loved well by the Lord of Hell,
      The hole of Erickstane brae.

  .   .   .   .   .

They found the rider at morn on the hill
      With his face upturned and cold,
And an awesome fear was in his eye
      As never a man has told.
And to this hour no word or power,
      Love nor honour nor dread,
Will lead a man by the waters wan
      To the moors of Erickstanehead.

The Strong Man Armed *(1895)*

First published in the *Glasgow University Magazine* 17 November 1897, it has also appeared in *Poems Scots and English* (1917), *A Book of Poetry* (1928), and the *John Buchan Journal*, Vol. I, No. 1 (1980). A verse is quoted in a *A Lodge in the Wilderness* (1906).

"Gift me guerdon and grant me grace,"
　　　Said the Lord of the North.
"Nothing I ask thee of gear or place
　　　Ere I get me forth.
Gift one guerdon to mine and me
　　　For the shade and the sheen."
　　.　　　.　　　.　　　.

"Ask and it shall be given unto thee,"
　　　Said Mary the Queen.

"May I never falter the wide world through,
　　　But stand in the gate:
May my sword bite sharp and my steel ring true
　　　At the ford and the strait:
Bide not on bed nor dally with song
　　　When the strife goeth keen;
This be my boon from the Gods of the strong!"
　　.　　.　　.　　.　　.　　.

　　　"Be it so," said the Queen.

"May I stand in the mist and the clear and the chill,
　　　In the cycle of wars,
In the brown of the moss and the grey of the hill
　　　With my eyes to the stars!
Gift this guerdon and grant this grace
　　　That I bid good e'en,
The sword in the hand and the foot to the race,
The wind in my teeth and the rain in my face!"
　　.　　.　　.　　.　　.　　.

　　　"Be it so," said the Queen.

Antiphilus of Byzantium   *(1895)*

Anth. Pal. ix. 546

A quotation from this poem is given in *A Lodge in the Wilderness* (1906). It later appeared in *Poems Scots and English* (1917).

Give me a mat on the deck,
  When the awnings sound to the blows of the spray,
And the hearthstones crack with the flames a-back
  And the pot goes bubbling away.
Give me a boy to cook my broth;
  For table a ship's plank lacking a cloth,
  And never a fork or knife;
And, after a game with a rusty pack,
The bo'sun's whistle to pipe us back —
  That's the fortune fit for a king,
  For Oh! I love common life!

Princess of the Shining Eyes   *(1895/1899)*

In *Unforgettable, Unforgotten* (1945) Anna Buchan (O.Douglas), introduces a poem which she attributes as having been written by John Buchan whilst he was at Oxford. It is untitled though the one given will identify it. The poem reads:

"We were two children, you and I,
Unkempt, unwatched, far-wandering, shy,
Trudging from morn with easy load,
While Faery lay adown the road . . .
Sometimes, on sunny summer's noon,
Our wearied feet got elfin shoon,
And we toiled up the hill so high
We seemed to knock against the sky,
While far above the clouds we heard
The singing of the snow-white Bird . . .

You in such lore were wondrous wise,
My princess of the shining eyes.
Our favour was the crimson Rose,
Our light the glow-worm's lamp, our ways
The Road the King of Errin goes,
And that is to the End of Days."

To Master Izaak Walton *(1896)*

This Epilogue is taken from a book of fishing poems *Musa Piscatrix* (1896). The poem was reprinted in *Fisherman's Verse* (1919), and in *An Angler's Garland of Fields, Rivers, and Other Country Contentments* (1920).

Master, I trow 'tis mony a year
Since last you fared a-fishing here,
Since first you cast your eager flies
Athwart the streams of Paradise.
And we, we love to read thy book
By placid stream and trickling brook,
When trout are scarce or winds are loud,
Or when the sky hath never a cloud.
But you are in a happier mead,
Where fish are never on the feed.

And, master, these are evil days
When scarce a man our art may praise.
For some they say 'tis most unfit
For bearded men in peace to sit,
And watch a meditative hook,
Or read a cheerful, pleasant book,
When they should to their work be hieing,
For time is short and all are dying.

And some they hold 'tis most unkind
Around the hook the silk to wind,
And hold a fish with barb or steel, —
As if, forsooth, a fish could feel.

38

But some there were both stout and hale
Who did not bow the knee to Baal.
Good Master Stoddart, now with God,
Full well he loved to walk the sod
On a fresh, westering April day
And see the sportive salmon play.

And the great singer of the north,
He loved by stream to wander forth;
He hated not the rod and line,
He called thee "Walton, sage, benign."
And some there be in London town,
Of bookish men, who often down
To the green country come to try
Their long-loved skill of fishery.

Why weary thee with idle praise,
Thou wanderer in Elysian ways?
Where skies are fresh aand fields are green,
And never dust nor smoke is seen,
Nor news sheets, nor subscription-lists,
Nor merchants, nor philanthropists.
For there the waters fall and flow
By flagrant banks, and still below
The great three-pounders rise and take
The 'palmer,' 'alder,' 'dun,' or 'drake.'
Now by that stream, if there you be,
I prithee keep a place for me.

A Journey of Little Profit *(1896)*

The verse first appeared introducing the short story 'A Journey of Little Profit', which appeared in *The Yellow Book* in April 1896 and later in the collection *Grey Weather* (1899).

The Devil he sang, the Devil he played
High and fast and free.
And this was ever the song he made
As it was told to me.

"Oh, I am the king of the air and the ground,
And lord of the seasons' roll,
And I will give you a hundred pound,
If you will give me your soul."

                              The Ballad of Grey Weather

Gibraltar   *(1897)*

'Gibraltar' was Buchan's unsuccessful contribution for the Newdigate Poetry Prize
written in his second year at Oxford. A hand-written pencil copy by Buchan is in the
National Library of Scotland and is published here for the first time.

Where Eastern waters, hot from sun-browned lands,
Long lost in isles and mazed on Afric sands,
Haste to the stern Atlantic, fierce and free
And find the deep unfathomable sea;
There stands a rick, above the shaken strait
Girdled with iron, the warder at the gate
Of the firm tracts of earth, immortal, high,
Wide to the swift winds out the glittering sky.
When from the Orient Dawn drives forth her car
Here first the shafts are flung, and when afar
The sun sets red and the soft daylight flies
On this bold front the mellow evening dies.
The seasons bring their dower, to all the lands,
When till and reap, to Spring with gen'rous hands
Gives of her plenty, summer adds her store
And Autumn brings her harvest evermore.
But this blunt crag recks not of change or time
Nor Winter brings decay nor June her prime,
But ageless, placid, her grey face she rears.
To meet the months, and spruce-like, take the years.
Unmoved, unchanged to face the tempests' war
The sun of noon and the lone evening-star.
The years fleet on, the nations strive and pass
The world grows old and in a darkling glass
Change leaves its' image, all is haunted, thick

With legends of lost days. But even as quick
At Springs' first blush, green mantles o'er the bough
Of the high-spending oak, so girt art thou
With memory of the cycles of all time
Age lies upon thee as the morning-rime
Of speech, the voiceless years find heritage
Thou art all clad in story; on thy page.

In the dim dawn of man when life was still
And remote as some untrodden hill
Whereon strange portents dwelled, and on each hand
Linked Unknown Doors above the golden land,
When seas were wide, and skies unnarrowed then
To the blind wondering world of wandering men
Thou marked the portal, where this narrow ken
Of parcelled shore ceased, and the dark beyond
Was thick with terrors. Oft the seaman conned
This chart of isles and longing looked again
To where below thy terrace yawned the main
And thought of how in his far Lycian town
The minstrel sang of lands beyond thy frown

The golden islets set in summer seas
Beyond thy Pillars, called of Herakles,
Of how some Greatheart, hot with youth, set sail
Loosed all his cords and drove before the gale,
Till some still morn he saw the yellow sands,
The golden apples and slim-ankled bands
Of ocean-maids, and last, his bride to be,
The light-tamed watcher of the waters, she
More fair in face than fair Persephone.
Fired with such word, the seaman quarrelled no more
Scorned his dull round, and loosing from the shore
Sailed to the evening, that in the suns path
He drove his course, and met the tempest's wrath
With front of rain, till after many days
And wanderings may in adventurous ways
When all his face with salt was crusted o'er
Wearied he sank, as never heretofore,
Fordone with toils of battle with the brine,

Then o'er the bows there flashed a gleaming line
Of surf-washed rocks and fields fresh-bathed in rains
Of cloud-capped hills o'ershadowing orchard plains
While sighed the airs ineffable, the breeze
That soft and low, lulls the Hesperides.

Hither the heroes came, the godlike race
Of seer divine, to whom a destined place
Lay in Olympus, doomed withal to toil
In this mid-world, to learn the battles' moil
And the swift shock of pain; in wrath and dearth
In flood and famine o'er the fortressed earth
To drink the dregs of their un-godlike truth
And he, the first, the mighty Herakles
When in fierce toil he crossed the Tamir seas.
Steered 'neath thy shadow, he the chief, the king,
Large-eyed, hood-pointed, girt and threatening.

The lustres poised, our charge, hot-foot with time
Laid grasping hands on men, no more sublime
They entered Argos, manned with fewer hands
Flit by the shores of the low summer lands.
On perilous quest unknown, nor more the sweep
Of man divine stirred the resounding deep,
Then flashed the gleam of gold from heart and head
Of the hozed warrior, fierce and helmeted.

Now shone the sun of morn on laden prow
Slow drifting with the tide beneath thy brow
Of pillared-rock; all thronged the deck with those
Hard to endure the battering war of woes.
On land and deep, keen-faced and wet with rain
Of sea and heaven, lushful of merchants' gain,
No pilgrims of the earth. In bays forlorn
Where from its hills is the rude Tamar torn
And all the land with winds is scarred and worn.
There cast thy anchor and unloose their bales
And earn bare need of the affronting gales,
Or haply on more distant quest and strange
They drive their wine when winds of winter range

In the affrighted North, and daylight lie
O'er half the year, and the last twilight die
In gleams dawn, by iron coasts they run
Where steely ice lies bare to the cold sun.
Till on some tiresome morn they scan the low
Ribbed plains of white which to the worlds' end go
And a lean white bear stalking in the snow.

They too have passed, and now from dawn to dawn
Flit forth ships, the loose-sailed galleys drawn
Henceforth the years are hot with war o'er thee
The strife of battle, the dark myriads flee,
Tarik, the moor, with all his warrior train
Gave thee his name; now the Saracen
Fled the Castillean, and in Fortunes' scales
By master charge, till the strong North prevails.
And Spain can Southward turn her page to thee
And know her empires' fortressed boundary.
From perils Mediterranean, East to West
They ceaseless sail on their unending quest,
Plenished with fruit of shore and fruit of sea
The high hills' birth, the gift of wood and lea
Easing the dower of earth, the toil of hands
To Rome, the enthroned lady of the lands.
Beneath its shade the Carthaginian sped
O'ersea to Spain and his dark spearmen led
Through the gaunt pass of the untrodden snow
To rich compassion needs, where soft and low
The sea winds sigh and the first roses blow.
Oft the proud Ceasars in their new-found sway
Led his mailed men to thee, when into the fray
The stout Herians rose, on Discords' wings
Flew off the walls of Mauritanian kings.

Anon they, too, the irremeable stream
Were ferried o'er, and like a sick mans' dream
The slow successors pass till that late hour
When in the settling of a sovran power
Then sawest the fleet bear the last leprous home
Toward the Northmen from the towers of Rome

Then through the summers of the hasting age
Comes the long train of toil-worn vassalage
Merchant and warrior, alone, and apart
Keen-eyed and thin, from labour in the mart
Of the worlds' cities, came the faithful hand
Who bore the immortal hope from land to land
Their will, their aid; girt with conquering sword
Couriers of peace, the envoy of the Lord.
Beneath thy brow the eternal tide of things
Bearing the cloak of war, pomp of kings
Flowed ceaseless, Northmen in heated galleys saw
Thy face at sunrise, and in lust and awe
Steered from the vexed Atlantic to the sea,
New hope and great their perplexity.
On the green current led the embattled lines
Of sun-browned moors to the soft land vines
The plain Castilian at the twilights' fall
Some dark sea-coves 'neath thy seaward wall
On slumbering town sailed like the whirlwinds' breath
And all thy rocks ring with the wail of death.

When the slow centuries brought the earth repose
And from the wreck of nature nations rose
And all men turned their eyes in tim'rous quest
From alien East to the untrodden West.
Then the tired seamen worn with pendrous years
Brought tidings marvellous to expectant ears
How o'er the desert of impetuous sea
A new world lay, unaltered, virgin, free
A land of gold, where Plenty, with full horn
Smiled at the eve, and ushered in the morn,
The old earth joyed at the speech of fresh-ploughed sod
And hailed the garden, wilderness of God
Then thy vexed straits saw the far-stretching fleets
Of men adventurous haste with straining sheets
With a fair wind behind, and whiles ver'lie how
The thunderous surging sea strained far and low,
The earnest of their toils. In the long train
Which, as the years fled and were calm again

Still ceaseless passed, the poor man and the great
Trod the same deck, the unbranded ship of state
Scared in the storms, and to the far-off ken
What layers of things, and strife of merchantmen.
Ah! who shall tell of the first sight of thee
Which dawned on way-worn exiles from o'ersea
Returning, all fractious with tempest strain
Or sick with gleam of green Mediterranean plain.
The long low level of the surgeless main.
When o'er the straits he saw thy barrier stand
And knew the watcher of his fatherland
Or haply the great galleons staggering on
Laden with spice and gold of Arizon
With all their faith thick-cloaked with stormy wrack
And a few English pirates at their back
While their great side shook to the North seas shock
Saw through the mist the brow of some high rock
And thanked their guardian saints and bore away
To the sure haven of thy o'er-shadowed bay.

And now the centuries brought thee alien kings
A folk who dwelled where the white ocean sings
The Northern tribes, a people great in war
The vagrants of the South, who near or far
By Arctic ice a'neath the southern star,
In desert muster or on the high hills' dome
Have set their play and called the wilds their home
A race of freemen, who through wind and wave
Were sworn to strive to glory or a grave.
Then all day long the toilsome battle rang
About thy base, and the shrill bullet sang
Around thy startled front, till the dread close
When o'er thy barrier leapt the alien foes,
And, fighting hard, set high their play on thee
Then, the embattled point of liberty
And soon, in turn, they too in after day,
Faced the attack of fleets, till all the bay
Was strewn with uncharted wrecks, or far away
Down the suns' path the shattered freemen sway
And the haunted eve broods upon the day.

But years have flown since the brave front of war
Looked on thy brow, and the hot bullets' scar
Washed with the dent of storms; slow years of peace
Laden with plentious dower of rich increase
Have passed and smiled upon thy tranquil lands
Now only artists do favour at their hands,
Lo thy bare face feels the winds and suns of Spring
Are vain as Winters' bouquet menacing,
The shock of war as the soft summers' rule
The pains of death as Fortune bountiful.
The earth is sick with toil and haste and heat
The dust of ages clog mans' hurrying feet.
He flits like Ariel forth o'er land and sea
And give no bounds to high timerity.
The ships go forth like locusts on the main,
Then sailors say they would return and seek again
Once more with unquenched hope and changeless zest
To face fresh toils, in all there is no rest,
For the whole earth must render up her hold,
Of close-held wealth, her secrets all are told
Her power in thrall, her beauty bright with gold.

Nay, yet not all, for the high hills are free
No law can lay its' bridle on the sea,
No winds which blow from the great roof of God
March the vain craft of man, the masters' rod.
No little passion stir the placid skies
Or the fame stains' inevitable eyes
'Tis but below the earth is thrall to man
And bears the markings of his little plan.
Strength, peace, disdain, and ever deep repose
Clothe the sharp eyes and veil the eternal snows.
So now thy dear lifes' noisy fervour flow.
No chattering huckster and the martial show
Colour and riot, toil and death or pain
Are thrust beneath as sad autumnal rain
But as the lone still morn when a red sun
Dawns on a moorland measureless where none
Hath dwelt, or shall dwell, and the air is thin
With utter silence, so a peace akin

Sits in thy ageless forehead. All may hope
Our little lessons, whence the feeble grope
To think he wots not; all the feverish lore,
Which he must seek and lose for evermore;
Was seen by thee in this eternal place
No dissent winds are brushed upon thy face.
Breathed on till morn, kissed of the West-wind low
Thou knowest the wisdom which no mortals know;
Thy scarred sea-front times' grim epitome,
Mistress of quiet in battle, silent, free.

Even as some guerdon, when the gods befriend,
Wrestles through strife to his appointed end.
And the high point of vantage gained, looks forth
And sees the world rush on, and knows the worth
Of its' frail honour, and himself can show
Safety or succour to the weak below
And there endures, in new lands common lot
No aid untried, no benefit forgot.
And while the toilers scan but his high seat
He in the watch-tower of his lone retreat
Looks from the clamour of terrestial wars
To the great peace which dwells among the stars.

From the Pentlands Looking North and South   *(1898)*

This poem was written while Buchan was an undergraduate at Oxford for an undergraduate society, The Horace Club. It first appeared in *The Book of the Horace Club*
(1901), Buchan's short story collection *The Moon Endureth* (1912), *Poems Scots and
English* (1917), *Northern Numbers, First Series* (1920), and *The Clearing House* (1946).

Around my feet the clouds are drawn
In the cold mystery of the dawn:
No breezes cheer, no guests intrude,
No mossy, mist-clad solitude:
When sudden down the steeps of sky
Flames a long, lightening wind. On high

The steel-blue arch shines clear, and far,
In the low lands where cattle are,
Towns smoke. And swift, a haze, a gleam, —
The Firth lies like a frozen stream,
Reddening with morn. Tall spires of ships,
Like thorns about the harbour's lips,
Now shake faint canvas, now, asleep,
Their salt, uneasy slumbers keep;
While, golden-grey, o'er kirk and wall
Day wakes in the ancient capital.

Before me lie the lists of strife,
The caravanserai of life,
Whence from the gates the merchants go
On the world's highways; to and fro
Sail laden ships; and in the street
The lone foot-traveller shakes his feet,
And in some corner by the fire
Tells the old tale of heart's desire.
There, there, from alien seas and skies
Comes the far-quested merchandise: —
Wrought silks of Khassa, Mocha's ware
Brown-tinted, fragrant, and the rare
Thin perfumes which the roses' breath
Has sought, immortal in her death:
Gold, gems and spice, and haply still
The red, rough largess of the hill,
Which takes the sun and bears the vines
In the blue misty Apennines.
And he who treads the cobbled street
To-day in the cold North may meet,
Come month, come year, the dusky East,
And share the Caliph's secret feast:
Or in the toil of wind and sun
Bear pilgrim-staff, forlorn, fordone,
Till o'er the steppe, athwart the sand,
There gleam the gates of Samarcand.
The ringing quay, the weathered face,
Fair skies, dusk hands, the ocean race,
The palm-girt isle, the ice-bound shore,

Gales and hot suns the wide world o'er,
Grey north, red south, and burnished west,
The goals of the old tireless quest,
Leap in the smoke, immortal, free,
Where shines yon morning fringe of sea.

I turn, and lo! the moorlands high
Lie still and frigid to the sky.
The film of morn is silver-grey
On the red heather, and away
Dim, distant, set in ribs of hill,
Green glens are shining, stream and mill,
Clachan and kirk and garden-ground,
All silent in the hush profound
Which haunts alone the hills' recess,
The antique home of quietness.
Nor to the folk can piper play
The tune of 'Hills and Far Away,'
For they are with them. Morn can fire
No peak of weary heart's desire,
Nor the red sunset flame behind
Some ancient ridge of longing mind.
For Arcady is here, around,
In lilt of stream, in the clear sound
Of lark and moorbird, in the old
Gay glamour of the evening gold.
And so the wheel of seasons moves
To kirk and market, to mild loves
And modest hates, and still the sight
Of brown kind faces, and when night
Draws dark around with age and fear
Theirs is the simple hope to cheer.
A land of peace where old romance
And ghostly shine of helm and lance
Still dwell by castled scarp and lea,
And the lost homes of chivalry.
And the good fairy folk, my dear,
Who speak for cunning souls to hear,
In nook of glen and bower of hill
Sing of the Happy Ages still.

O Thou to whom man's heart is known,
Grant me my morning orison.
Grant me the rover's path — to see
The dawn arise, the daylight flee,
In the far wastes of sand and sun!
Grant me with venturous heart to run
On the old highway where in pain
And ecstasy man strives amain,
Conquers his fellows, or, too weak,
Finds the great rest which wanderers seek.
Grant me the joy of wind and brine,
The zest of food, the taste of wine,
The fighter's strength, the echoing strife,
The high tumultuous lists of life —
May I ne'er lag, nor hapless fall,
Nor weary at the battle-call.

But when the even brings surcease
Grant me the happy moorland peace;
That in my heart's depth ever lie
That ancient land of heath and sky;
Where the old rhymes and stories fall
In kindly, soothing pastoral.
There in the hills grave silence lies,
And Death himself wears friendly guise,
There be my lot, my twilight stage,
Dear city of my pilgrimage.

John Burnet of Barns *(1898)*

Buchan's second novel *John Burnet of Barns* was published in 1898 and is set in both Scotland and the Low Countries. In the story Marjory Veitch is said to have a wonderful singing voice. She is asked by John Burnet to sing to him and he 'set down the words as she sang them':

> "Oh, if my love were sailor-bred,
>   And fared afar from home,
> In perilous lands, by shoal and sands,
>   If he were sworn to roam,
> Then, oh, I'd hie me to a ship,
>   And sail upon the sea,
> And keep his side in wind and tide,
>   To bear him company.

> "And if he were a soldier gay,
>   And tarried from the town,
> And sought in wars, through death and scars,
>   To win for him renown,
> I'd place his colours in my breast,
>   And ride by moor and lea,
> And win his side, there to abide,
>   And bear him company.

> "For sooth a maid, all unafraid,
>   Should by her lover be,
> With wile and art to cheer his heart,
>   And bear him company."

Later John Burnet, nearing home after his journeying, heard a "faint melody, the voice of a girl singing":

> "First shall the heavens want starry light,
>   The seas be robbed of their waves;
> The day want sun, the sun want bright,
>   The night want shade, and dead men graves;
>   The April, flowers and leaf and tree,
>   Before I false my faith to thee,
>   To thee, to thee."

"First shall the tops of highest hills
  By humble plains be overpry'd;
And poets scorn the Muses' quills,
  And fish forsake the water-glide;
    And Iris lose her colour'd weed
    Before I fail thee at thy need."

"First direful Hate shall turn to Peace,
  And Love relent in deep disdain;
And Death his fatal stroke shall cease,
  And Envy pity every pain;
    And Pleasure mourn, and Sorrow smile,
    Before I talk of any guile."

"First Time shall stay his stayless race,
  And Winter bless his brows with corn;
And snow bemoisten July's face,
  And Winter, Spring and Summer mourn."

"First shall the heavens want starry light,
  The seas be robbed of their waves;
The day want sun, the sun want bright,
  The night want shade, and dead men graves;
    The April, flowers and leaf and tree,
    Before I false my faith to thee."

To the Adventurous Spirit of the North   *(1898)*

This short poem appeared as an introduction to John Buchan's Newdigate Prize Poem
of 1898. In a manuscript supplied by the Yale University Library, New Haven,
Connecticut, this title is given as *'Verus Lettorum Spiritus Aut Borealis Afflatus, Ut
Scripsit Claudianus'*.

Born of the grey sea-shroud,
  Born of the wind and spray,
Where the long hills sink to the morning cloud
  And the mist lies low on the bay:
Child of the stars and the skies,

Child of the dawn and the rain,
The April shining of ladies' eyes,
    And the infinite face of pain!

Seal on the hearts of the strong,
    Guerdon, thou, of the brave,
To nerve the arm in the press of the throng,
    To cheer the dark of the grave. —
Far from the heather hills,
    Far from the misty sea. —
Little it irks where a man may fall
    If he fall with his heart on thee.

To fail and not to faint,
    To strive and not to attain,
To follow the Path to the end of days
    Is the burden of thy strain.
Daughter of hope and tears,
    Mother, thou of the free,
As it was in the beginning of years
    And evermore shall be.

"And this was the word of the wise women who spin among the hills:
'Counsel for the true-hearted: to follow the Path the King of Errin rides,
which is the road to the end of days.' "

The Pilgrim Fathers *(1898)*

At Oxford University, and at his third attempt, this entry won the the Newdigate Prize
for John Buchan.

Behold your heritage, your land of quest!
Long have ye sought, near comes the hour of rest.
Go, children, forth with scrip and staff, and far
In toil of tempest and the dust of war
Seek your continuing city. Seek and pray,
Gird ye and strive and faint not on the way.
God be your strength, your buckler and your sword.
Then forth my sons! Who followeth with the Lord?

What came you out to seek? A path of flowers,
A sleep-lulled valley and the silent bowers
Of sinless Edens, where the slumbrous days
Slip past unheeded, and the noon-day blaze
Is cheered by zephyrs born of the warm South,
And grapes of Eschol cool the parched mouth?
Thirst ye for these, or for the soft green fold
Of summer hills, where like a chart unrolled
Lie town and hamlet girt with woody lea
And dewy lawns and the unchanging sea?
Long leagues of ocean whitening to the sky
Sever our path from lands of infancy.
Our homes are lost us, lost the song and rhyme,
The hearth's red glow, the stories of old time,
Corn on the holm-land, fruit upon the tree
And the far-hallowed seats of memory.
But clear our faith as April's first sunrise,
Which bursts the dark and cheers the lonely eyes:
No faltering shakes their steadfastness whose ways
Lie on the King's Path to the end of days.

Ay! on the King's Path! Men have toiled and bled
On the old quest; and we, with the king-like head,
Fronting the sword of monarchs and their scorn,
Have dared their terrors; and have trod forlorn
A prouder path than captains of great might
Fair with the pomp and panoply of fight.
Ours is the weary way, which knows no end
Save with the coming of great Death, the Friend;
Ours is the ageless day which sees no close
Till the last sunset bring the set of woes.
Each moment throngs with strife, the lists are built,
The untiring foe is near to ride a-tilt.
Our arm is never slack, our eyes are sore
With dust of tumult surging evermore:
While, like a clarion, rings the immortal word,
"Not peace I bring, not comfort, but a sword."

What came you out to seek? A wilderness
Untilled, untouched, a home of loneliness

Set in some forest haunt whose trackless deeps
Darken the shining dawn? The wild deer sleeps
On fields which ye must sow, and by the spring,
Which now is stirred but by the mere-fowl's wing,
The austere chant of thanksgiving must rise
And rugged hearths smoke to the morning skies.
Ours was the quiet lot, where each new day
Brought the old duties. Clear our passage lay
'Mid sunlit meadows; smoothly through each stage
Life's journey ran, an easy pilgrimage.
So fond our hopes; but sudden came the frost,
Untimely, bitter, and our peace was lost.
"Quit ye like men" — Who wills it, let him hear,
And his the faith which casteth out all fear!
Steeled in his heart to bid the long good-night,
Unblenched he fronts the desert and the fight.

What came ye out to seek? Regret and tears
And the long void of immemorial years?
Not so, my children. Shall a man be upbraid
The Lord who him and all his joys hath made?
He, the poor creature, born of grief and shame,
A clot of dust, a spark of heavenly flame!
Shall he by seeking find the majesty
That plants its footsteps on the hills and sea?
For man the servant's task, the bond-slave's place,
To toil and see not of his labour's grace.
The wide creation travaileth in pain;
And shall the pigmy in his griefs complain?
Our lot hath blessings. Fare we near or far,
Our quiet mind shall light its evening star;
Wearied with toil, our bed in desert lands
Shall be the old green couch not made with hands;
The twilights cool our mead when day is done,
And the sweet comfort of the morning sun.
For us, unasked, the autumn fruit shall glow,
The loud fire crackle when the winters blow.

Ours the forgotten life, the elder birth
Of men unwearied in the ancient earth.
Though o'er our path the wrack of battle roll,

55

No wars perplex the sabbath of our soul.
What though the body be a sacrifice
To the fierce sun or the inclement skies,
The lurking wild beast or the savage king,
We are not sad for all their threatening.
Life is not meat nor drink nor raiment fine,
But a man's courage and the fire divine.
Yea, hearts insurgent 'mid the obedient crowd
We ever bore, and walked upon the loud
And perilous road of honour. Man may fall
And yet attain. And he who hears the call,
And tracks the gleam through rock and wood and fen,
Haps on the treasure hid from petty men.
And as in desert sands the holy race,
Fleeing from Egypt to their destined place,
Nursing their hope through pity and distress,
Set up a shrine amid the wilderness;
So we, lone outlaws in these evening lands,
Yet to the past hold forth unfaltering hands,
And bear old faiths in vanguard of our wars,
And set our eyes upon the ancient stars.

Then forth my children! lo! the gold of dawn
Burns on yon eastern hill; the grassy lawn,
The tangled forests, fire with morn; the beams
Of a new sun fall on the virgin streams.
Clear sings the bird of hope, and far and nigh
Winds wake the embattled silence of the sky.
The shining footprints of the light to be
Tremble and glow along the inviolate sea.
The world awakes for you, the young the strong;
And we, the old, who wait and wait not long
On the last call, give you a glad God-speed,
True heart in peril and stout arm in need,
While with untroubled eyes we watch and pray
Till the brief dark that fadeth into day.

56

The Gipsy's Song to the Lady Cassilis   *(1898)*

The poem was published first in the *Glasgow University Magazine* (1898). It also appears in *The Book of the Horace Club* (1901), *The Living Age* (1901), *The Moon Endureth* (1912), *Poems Scots And English* (1917), *Northern Numbers* (*Second Series* 1921), and *The Clearing House* (1946).

'Whereupon the Faas, coming down from the Gates of Galloway, did so bewitch my lady that she forgot husband and kin, and followed the tinkler's piping.'

Chap-book of the Raid of Cassilis

The door is open wide, my love,
   The air is bright and free;
Adown the stair, across the hall,
   And then — the world and me;
The bare grey bent, the running stream,
   The fire beside the shore;
And we will bid the hearth farewell,
   And never seek it more,
               My love,
   And never crave it more.

And you will wear no silken gown,
   No maid shall bind your hair;
The yellow broom shall be your gem,
   Your braid the heather rare.
Athwart the moor, adown the hill,
   Across the world away; —
The path is long for happy hearts
   That sing to greet the day,
               My love,
   That sing to greet the day.

And at the last no solemn stole
   Shall on thy breast be laid;
No mumbling priest shall speed thy soul,
   No charnel vault thee shade.
But by the shadowed hazel copse,
   Aneath the greenwood tree,
Where airs are soft and waters sing,

57

Thou'lt ever sleep by me,
My love,
Thou'lt ever sleep by me.

In the later publication of *The Book of the Horace Club* (1901) the poem contains an additional verse and some minor differences, it is given below in full.

'Whereupon the Faas, coming down from the gates of Galloway, did so bewitch my lady that she forgat husband and kin, and followed the tinkler's piping.'

(Chap-book of the Raid of Cassilis)

The door is open to the wall,
The air is bright and free;
Adown the stair, across the hall,
And then — the world and me;
The bare grey bent, the running stream,
The fire beside the shore,
And we will bid the hearth farewell,
And never seek it more,
My love,
And never crave it more.

And you shall wear no silken gown,
No maid shall bind your hair;
The yellow broom shall be your gem,
Your braid the heather rare.
Athwart the moor, adown the hill,
Across the world away;
The path is long for happy hearts
That sing to greet the day,
My love,
That sing to greet the day.

When morning cleaves the eastern grey
And the lone hills are red;
When sunsets light the evening way
And birds are quieted;

In autumn noon and spring-tide dawn,
    By hill and dale and sea,
The world shall sing its ancient song
    Of hope and joy for thee,
                    My love,
    Of hope and joy for thee.

And at the last no solemn stole
    Shall on thy breast be laid;
No mumbling priest shall speed thy soul,
    No charnel vault thee shade.
But by the shadowed hazel copse,
    Aneath the greenwood tree
Where airs are soft and waters sing,
    Thou'lt ever sleep by me,
                    My love,
    Thou'lt ever sleep by me.

ॐ   ॐ   ॐ

Ballad for Grey Weather   *(1898)*

This poem is printed in *Grey Weather* (1899), where it is dated 1 April 1898. It has also appeared in *The Book of the Horace Club* (1901), and in *Poems Scots and English* (1917) where it is entitled 'The Singer'.

Cold blows the drift on the hill,
    Sere is the heather,
High goes the wind and shrill,
    Mirk is the weather.
Stout be the front I show,
    Come what the gods send!
Plaided and girt I go
    Forth to the world's end.

My brain is the stithy of years,
    My heart the red gold
Which the gods with sharp anguish and tears

Have wrought from the old.
In the shining first dawn o' the world
   I was old as the sky, —
The morning dew on the field
   Is no younger than I.

I am the magician of life,
   The hero of runes;
The sorrows of eld and old strife
   Ring clear in my tunes.
The sea lends her minstrel voice,
   The storm-cloud its grey;
And ladies have wept at my notes,
   Fair ladies and gay.

My home is the rim of the mist,
   The ring of the spray.
The hart has his corrie, the hawk has her nest,
   But I — the Lost Way.
Come twilight or morning, come winter or spring,
   Come leisure, come war,
I tarry not, I, but my burden I sing
   Beyond and afar.

I sing of lost hopes and old kings,
   And the maids of the past.
Ye shiver adread at my strings,
   But ye bear them at last.
I sing of vain quests and the grave, —
   Fools tremble, afraid.
I sing of hot life, and the brave
   Go forth, undismayed.

I sleep by the well-head of joy
   And the fountain of pain.
Man lives, loves, and fights, and then is not, —
   I only remain.
Ye mock me and hold me to scorn, —

I seek not your grace.
Ye gird me with terror — forlorn,
I laugh in your face.

The Singer *(1898)*

A poem under this title appears in *Poems Scots and English* (1917), but it is the same as the one above entitled 'Ballad for Grey Weather' which appeared in *Grey Weather* (1899).

Lady Keith's Lament *(1898)*

This poem appeared in '*A Lost Lady of Old Years*' (1899).

> "A' are gane, the gude, the kindly,
>   Low in the moss and far on the sea,
> Men o' the North, men o' the muirlands,
>   Brave to battle and laith to flee.
> I was aince a lady o' pride,
>   High my hame abune the heather;
> Now my silken gown I tine,
>   I maun fare in wind and weather."
>
> "Kin and kith in weary battle
>   By stranger waters across the faem
> Fell, and dying had mind o' sweet Argos,
>   The man of auld and the hills of hame
> The ship is rocking by the pier,
>   The hour draws nigh when we maun pairt.
> Then fare thee weel, my loved, my dear,
>   Bide I canna, though breaks my hert."
>
> "But though I now maun wander dowie,
>   And drap the tear on cheek sae pale,
> Yet shall our dule be turned to joy,
>   For God maun let the richt prevail.

My father was a guid lord's son,
        My mither was an earl's daughter;
And I'll be Lady Keith again
        The day the King comes ower the water."

ॐ   ॐ   ॐ

The Soldier of Fortune (1899)

This poem first appeared in *The Book of the Horace Club* (1901), and it also appeared in *The Student*, an Edinburgh University publication, during that same year. However, when printed in *Poems Scots and English* (1917), it is recorded as being written during 1899. It was printed later in *Our Tounis College* (1928).

I have seen thy face in the foray, I have heard thy voice in the fray,
        When the stars shrunk in the silence or the great midnights blew;
Men have worn their steel-blades, seeking by night and day,
        Selling their souls for the vain dreams, — I have followed the true.
Frosts have dulled the scabbard, suns have furrowed the thong,
        And the great winds of the north-west have steeled the vagrant eye;
So through the world I wander, haggard and fierce and strong,
        Seeking the goal I see not, toiling I tell not why.

I have loved all good things, song and foray and wine,
        The hearth's red glow at the even, the gladsome face of a friend,
The sun and snows of the hill-lands, the sting of the winter's brine,
        Dawn and noon and the twilight, day and the day-light's end.
I have ridden the old path, ridden it fierce and strong,
        By camp and city and moorland and the grey face of the sea;
Wrath abides on my forehead, but at my heart a song,
        The ancient wayfaring ballad, the royal chaunt of the free.

For ever in cloud or May-tide thy voice has been in my ear,
        In the quivering mists of battle thy face has shone like a star;
Never the steel ranks broke when the Lord sent forth His fear,
        But thy hand has held my bridle and girt my soul for war.
I am broken and houseless, lost my clan and my name,
        A stranger treads on my homelands, no heart remembereth me.
But be thou my portion, lady of stars and flame,
        Little I ask of the red gold, having the winds and thee.

The Last Song of Oisin *(1901)*

First published in *The Book of The Horace Club* (1901), a book of poems written and collected over the period of 1898 to 1901, by members of the Oxford club, and founded by John Buchan. Only 500 copies were printed and this particular poem has not appeared elsewhere.

Here is the cold, and there the sun and spring-tide,
    Here the grey dunes, and there the meads of peace,
Here the dim silence, there the joys of song-tide,
    Dull longing here, and pain that shall not cease.
Lo! I am wrinkled, old, and worn unsightly,
    Weary my step and faint my faltering knee,
Yet was I joyful once, and blithe, and knightly,
    In the lost lands adown the western sea.

From hut and hall the little peoples hasten:
    Crooked they come, and fickle in their ways:
They toil and sweat with weary breath to chasten
    The niggard earth through melancholy days.
And black-stoled men with dirge and chant assail them,
    And pedlar monarchs fatten on their woe.
Then at the even, when their sinews fail them,
    From the great toil to the great dark they go.

I was a lord and prince in the Far Islands,
    Where in the seas the dawn and twilight die,
Sweet with the winds of morn, the scent of highlands,
    The blush of fruit, the gold of western sky.
There dwell the kings who rode the kingly questing,
    The bards who chanted in the long ago,
There the high warriors from the battle resting
    Drink the full cups which the immortals know.

Among the lilied fields of the Hereafter
    Dwell they whom all men sought the wide world through,
Star-eyed, bright-tressed, before whose tears and laughter
    Steel turned to wax, and rosemary to rue.
More faint and far than elfin bells in May-time
    Comes their dear voice across the sundering snow,

And through the mist and sleet of this dark daytime
   Their rose-fringed garments trail and gleam and go.

I shiver! Lo! the little peoples cluster,
   Poor twisted things that stare and, wondering, flee.
'Tis even; from afar the toilers muster;
   A little bell rings by the cold grey sea.
They laugh and flaunt among their barren places,
   Poor joyless mirth, poor passionless base tears!
A coward death grins from their pallid faces,
   For truth has fled with the old kingly years.

My breath is heavy. Haste thou, Death the master,
   Come with the great winds from the shoreless deep!
Carry me far into the hills, O! faster,
   Through white-fanged pass to the still place of sleep.
Snow blinds my eyes: I faint: a light is glowing:
   The last shrill music in the tempest rings.
And the great midnight, wide and wild and blowing,
   Gathers my heart into its wandering wings.

The Semitic Spirit Speaks   *(1902/1903)*

This poem, in a hand-written draft, is in the National Library of Scotland. The first page
is headed Land Department, Pretoria, and it is assumed it was written whilst John
Buchan was serving with Lord Milner, High Commissioner for South Africa between
August 1901 and August 1903.

Before was made the earth and sea
Or Adam sprang from God his sire,
Of equal parts of guile and mire
The Lord in jest created me.

Though men may curse and men may laud,
Even now as when the world was young,
Inserting in my cheek my tongue,
I am the oldest kind of Fraud.

For me the courage of the lare,
The humour of the affair is mine,
My tastes are even of the swine,
But I'm a multi-millionaire.

I own no fatherland nor laws;
The watchword of the world I hear,
A pleasant music in my ear,
For I can turn them to my cause.

I float their play above my tents,
I spur the people on to fight,
And when they perish in the night
I turn me to my tent for cents.

But if in spite of all my care
Some breath of danger came to me,
Why, then, I sail across the sea
And buy a house in Grosvenor Square.

And when at length this body dies,
The Lord will never say me no.
With thirty thousand, pounds or so
I'll buy a pass for Paradise.

Ours were the jobs of elder years, —
Our lady of the Snows and Tears,
Angus the Subtle, Circean grey,
And Morag of the Misty Day.
You in such lore were woundrous wise,
My princess of the shining eyes.
Our favour was the Crimson Rose.
Our light the glow-worms' lamp, our ways
The Road the King of Errin goes,
And that is to the End of Days.

And now — ah, now our paths have strayed
Far from the happy upland shade,
For we have grown so old, so old,
And I am stiff and you are cold.

Your hair is autumn-brown, your face
Fair with your old inviolate grace.
But now, too clever, you and I,
For simple earth and simple sky
Must toil and fret and build our plans,
Matching our strength with God's and man's.
So be it, dear. If to achieve,
To stand above the crowd and leave
Old common raptures to the base,
If to press ceaseless in the race,
Be happiness, then we may win
To that triumphant sanhedrim.

But at last may it not fall
That, from our watch-towers scanning all,
Our work, our hope, our labour done,
Our little art beneath the sun.
The petty fame which blinds our eyes,
Our transient philosophies,
There rankle in our hearts a sting?
May it not hap that we shall fling
Our gold aside as earth and dross,
And mourn irrevocable loss?
God knoweth dear, for at the door
I hear an echo evermore,
Chill as the chill October rain,
"Can ye attain, can ye attain?"

Midian's Evil Day[1] (1904)

Taken from *Poems Scots and English* (1917). Buchan introduces this poem by reference to a letter from one Alexander Cargill, Elder of the Kirk of the Remnant in the vale of Wae, to the Reverend Murdo Mucklethraw, Minister of the aforesaid Kirk, about the Great Case argued in the House of Lords.

Dear Reverend Sir, — I take my pen
   To tell yon great occasion when
We garred our licht shine afore men,
      Yea, far and wide,
And smote the oppressor but and ben
      For a' his pride.

Yoursel', ye mind, was far frae weel —
A cauld we catch't at Kippenshiel,
Forbye rheumatics in your heel —
         And thus it came,
Fou though ye were o' holy zeal,
         Ye stopped at hame.

For me, my lamin'-time was bye,
The muirland hay was nane sae high,
The men were thrang, the grund was dry,
         Sae when ye spak,
And bade me gang and testify,
         I heldna back.

Wi' dowie hert I left that morn,
Reflectin' on the waefu' scorn
The Kirk man thole, her courts forlorn,
         Her pillars broke,
While Amalek exalts his horn,
         And fills his poke,

I pondered the mischances sair
The Lord had garred puir Scotland bear
Frae English folk baith late and ear'
         Sin' Flodden year
To the twae beasts at Carlisle fair
         I bocht ower dear.

If true religion got a fa'
Frae her auld courts and guid Scots law,
What hope o' succour far awa'
        'Mang godless chiels,
Whae at the Word sae crousely craw
        And fling their heels.

As weel expect the Gospel sap 'ill
Rise in uncovenantit thrapple
As saw a ploom to raise an apple,
        Or think a soo
Fleein' aloft on the hoose-tap 'ill
        Sit like a doo.

I like an owl in desert was,
When to the coorts I buid to pass,
Amang the crood to hear the Cause.
        Nae freend I saw, —
Juist some auld lads set oot in raws
        And belchin' law.

But ane sat cockit in atween,
A wee man but as gleg's a preen:
A walth o' sense was in his een
        And foreheid massy.
"The Chancellor," I was tellt, when keen
        I speired whae was he.

Wi' prayerfu' mind I watched the stert
While Maister Johnston[2] played his pairt,
And sune I fand my anxious hert
        Gie a great loup.
"Yon Chancellor the ungodly's cairt,"
        I said, "will coup."

O sir, that day I kent indeed
There's men o' worth across the Tweed,
Men whae are steadfast in the creed
        As Moses sel',

Men whae the Word o' God can read
      And cling to Hell.

I thocht they were a careless race,
Decked oot in cauld Erastian claes,
Whae traivelled a' in slippery ways,
      Whase thochts were vain:
But noo I ken they've gifts and grace
      E'en like oor ain.

A Lowden chiel[3] — black be his tryst! —
A wise-like man, but ill advised,
Led on the hosts o' Antichrist,
      And threepit bauld,
That man could never back be wysed
      To Calvin's fauld.

He made the yett o' Heaven sae wide
The veriest stirk could get inside:
Puffed up he was wi' warldly pride
      And fou o' German,
Quotin' auld pagans for his guide
      And sic-like vermin.

He fuecht wi' Prophets, jouked wi' Psalms,
He got his legs clean ower the trams,
He garred th' Apostles skip like rams
      Tae dae his biddin's:
Oor auld Confessions were but shams,
      Their loss guid riddance.

God foreordained some men to Hell —
Granted, but man can please himsel'
Up to a point — and if I dwell
      Mair on free-will
Than on election, I do well,
      A Christian still.

"For these are mysteries," quo' he,
"Whereon nae twae men can agree,
And sae it's richt for you and me —

> The thing's sae kittle —
Ane to consider half a lee, —
> Whilk — maitters little.

"It's a'," he said, "confusion wild;
In siccan things the best's a child;
Some walk an ell and some a mile;
> But never fear,
Thae doots will a' be reconciled
> In higher sphere.

"Therefore a kirk, whase lamps are bright,
Bequeathed by auld divines o' might,
Can fling them tapsalteerie quite,
> And think nae shame;
For white is black and black is white,
> It's a' the same."

But what availed his carnal lear
Against a man o' faith and prayer?
As through the thristles gangs the share
> And dings them doun,
E'en sae the Chancellor cleft him fair
> Frae heel to croun.

He pinned him wi' the Bible words,
He clove at him wi' Calvin's swirds,
He garred him loup aboot the boards
> Wi' muckle mense,
And bund him wi' the hempen cords
> O' plain guid sense.

"Threep as ye please, It's clear to me,
Whither or no' the twae agree,
Baith doctrines were appoint to be
> The Kirk's chief pillar.
If ane ye like to leave," says he,
> "Ye leave the siller."

Oh, wi' what unction he restored
The auld commandments o' the Lord,

Confoonded Bashan's nowt that roared,
    And 'stablished Hell!
Knox was nae soonder in the Word
    Nor Calvin's sel'.

I'll no' deny yon Lowden chiel
Was gleg as ony slippery eel,
For twae-three men frae Kippensheil
    Begood to waver;
I half inclined to doot the Deil
    A' through his claver.

But when a man o' faith and power
Uprose, he couldna bide an hour:
The weakest's doots were tided ower
    Anither towmont.
The Kirk stood firm as auld stane tower
    Wi' safe endowment.

  .   .   .   .   .   .

I hae a bull, a noble breed,
A shorthorn wi' a massy heid,
Wi' quarters fine and coat o' reid:
    On ilka lea
Frae Thurso to the banks o' Tweed
    He bears the gree.

I ca'ed him Begg[4] the same's his sire;
But noo for sign to a' the shire
O' yon great day when frae the mire
    Our feet we bore,
His name shall be in field and byre
    "The Chancellor."

Buchan includes the following footnotes:

1 The occasion of these verses requires a note. The union in 1900 of the Free Church of Scotland and the United Presbyterian Church led to secession of certain congregations of the former, who called themselves the Free Church, and maintained that the union involved a departure from the principles of that church and a breach of the conditions under which certain properties were held. They brought an action to establish their right to these properties, as the sole remaining repository of Free Church principles. This action was decided against the claimants in the Scottish courts, but, on appeal, the House of Lords, under the guidance of Lord Halsbury (then Lord Chancellor), reversed the decision.
2 Mr Henry Johnston, KC, of the Scots Bar (afterwards Lord Johnston), led for the appellants.

3 The leading counsel for the respondent was Mr R.B. Haldane (MP for East Lothian), afterwards Lord Chancellor of England.
4 A famous Free Church divine of the old school.

The Song of the Sea Captain   *(1905)*

This first appeared in *A Beggar's Wallet* (1905) and was included in *Poems Scots and English* (1917).

John Buchan introduces this poem by referring to Diego d'Alboquerque, who was the brother of the great Alphonso, a knight of the Portuguese Order of Jesus Christ. Having landed on the coast north of Zanzibar, he wandered into the Abyssinian Highlands where he saw and fell in love with Melissa, the daughter of Prester John and cousin to the Lady of Tripoli *(la princesse lointaine)*. Diego was slain off Goa in the great fight with the Sultan of Muscat.

> I sail a lone sea captain
>   Around the southern seas;
> Worn as my cheek, the flag of Christ
>   Floats o'er me on the breeze.
> By green isle and by desert,
>   By little white-walled town,
> To west wind and to east wind
>   I lead my galleons down.
>
> I know the black south-easter,
>   I know the drowsy calms
> When the slow tide creeps shoreward
>   To lave the idle palms.
> Of many a stark sea battle
>   The Muslim foe can tell,
> When their dark dhows I sent to crabs
>   And their dark souls to hell.
>
> Small reck have I of Muslim
>   Small reck of winds and seas,
> The waters are my pathway
>   To bring me to my ease.

The dawns that burn above me
   Are torches set to light
My footsteps to a garden
   Of roses red and white.

     .   .   .   .   .   .

Five months we stood from Lagos,
   While, scant of food and sleep,
We tracked da Gama's highroad
   Across the Guinea deep.
All spent we were with watching
   When, ghostly as a dream,
The Bona Esoeranza cape
   Rose dark upon the beam.

Then by the low green inlets
   We groped our passage forth,
Outside the shallow surf-bars
   We headed for the north.
Sofala gave us victual,
   Inyaka ease and rest,
But of the wayside harbours
   I loved Melinda best.

'Twas on a day in April,
   The feast of Rosaly,
We beached our weary vessels,
   Cried farewell to the sea,
And with ten stout companions
   And hearts with youth made bold
We sought the inland mountains
   Of which our fathers told.

No chart had we or counsel
   To guide our weary feet,
To north and west we wandered
   In drought and dust and heat,
Till o'er the steaming tree-tops
   We saw the far-off dome
Of mystic icy mountains,
   And knew the Prester's home.

Nine days we clomb the foothills,
  Nine days the mountain wall,
Sheer cliff and ancient forest
  And fretted waterfall;
And on the tenth we entered
  A meadow cool and deep,
And in the Prester's garden
  We laid us down to sleep.

Long time we fared like princes
  In palaces of stone,
For never guest goes cheerless
  Who meets with Prester John;
Where woodlands mount to gardens
  And gardens climb to snows
And wells of living water
  Sing rondels to the rose.

And there among the roses,
  More white and red than they,
There walked the gleaming lady,
  The princess far away.
Dearer her golden tresses
  Than the high pomp of wars,
And deep and still her eyes as lakes
  That brood beneath the stars.

There walked we and there spoke we
  Of things that may not cease,
Of life and death and God's dear love
  And the eternal peace.
For in that shadowed garden
  The world has grown so small
That one white girl in one white hand
  Could clasp and hold it all.

I craved the Prester's blessing,
  I kissed his kingly hand:
"Too soon has come the parting
  From this fair mountain land.

But shame it were for Christian knight
   To take his leisure here
When o'er the broad and goodly earth
   The Muslim sends his fear.

"I go to gird my sword on,
   To drive my fleets afar,
To court the wrath of tempests,
   The dusty toils of war.
But when my vows are ended,
   Then, joyous from the fray,
I come to claim my lady,
   The princess far away."

  .   .   .   .   .   .

I sail a lone sea captain
   Across the southern seas;
Worn as my cheek, the flag of Christ
   Still flaunts upon the breeze.
By green isle and by desert,
   By little white-walled town,
To west wind and to east wind
   I lead my galleons down.

But in the starkest tempest,
   And where the drowsy heats,
Where on the shattered coral
   The far-drawn breaker beats:
In seas of dreaming water,
   And in the wind-swept spray,
I see my snow-white lady,
   The princess far away.

Sometimes in inland places
   We march for weary days,
Where thorns parch in the noontide
   Or the fens are dark with haze; —
For me 'tis but a march of dreams,
   For ever, clear and low,
I hear cool waters falling
   In the garden of the snow.

Small reck have I of Muslim,
　　Small reck of sands or seas;
The wide world is my pathway
　　To lead me to my ease.
The dawns that burn above me
　　Are torches set to light
My footsteps to a garden
　　Of roses red and white.

A Lodge in the Wilderness　　*(1906)*

In Buchan's discussion novel about Empire, *The Lodge in the Wilderness*, friends of the
millionaire, Mr Francis Carey, have assembled at his retreat in Musuru, high above the
African veldt. During the first evening dinner Carey explains it is no ordinary house
party, but an occasion to 'examine ourselves and find the reason of that faith which is
in us.' Afterwards Hugh Somerville, modelled on Buchan himself, is joined by Lady
Flora Brune on the lawn and she reads him some poetry.

"Rests not the wild-deer in the park,
　　The wild-foul in the pen,
Nor nests the heaven-aspiring lark
　　Where throng the prints of men.
He who the King's Path once hath trod
　　Stays on in slumbrous isle,
But seeks where blow the winds of God
　　His lordly domicile.

Where 'neath the red-rimmed Arctic sun
　　The ice-bound whaler frets,
Where in the morn the salmon run
　　Far-shining to the nets;
Where young republics pitch their tents
　　Beside the Western wave,
And set their transient Presidents
　　As targets for the brave;

Where through th' illimitable plains
　　Nigerian currents flow,

76

And many a wily savage brains
   His unsuspecting foe;
Where gleam the lights of shrine and joss,
   From some far isle of blue,
Where screams beneath the Southern Cross
   The lonely cockatoo;

(The last word may be "caribou". Marjory wasn't sure whether a caribou or
a cockatoo was likely to scream the most.)

Where in the starlit Eastern night
   The dusky dervish sleeps,
Where the loan lama waits the light
   On Kanchenjunga's steeps;
Where Indian rajahs quaff their pegs
   And chase the listless flies,
Where mazed amid a pile of kegs
   Th' inebriate trader lies;

There, o'er the broad and goodly earth,
   Go seek th' imperial soul.
Broken the barriers of his birth,
   Th' eternal heavens his goal.
In wind or wet, in drink or debt,
   Steeled heart no fate can stir,
He is the Render of the Net,
   Th' Immortal Wanderer."

Later in the book another untitled poem is recited which is described as
"a kind of dialogue between Youth and the Spirit of Art".

YOUTH

Angel of love and light and truth,
   In whose deep eyes the stars are set,
And in whose calm unchanging youth
   The mysteries of the world have met,

What means thy forward-beckoning hand,
  The steadfast brow, the enraptur'd gaze?
They point me to a lonely land —
  I cannot pierce the twilight haze.

With thee of old I walked at noon.
  In gardens where the airs were kind,
And from thy lips I read the rune
  Of joy in every wave and wind.

We roamed blue hills of far romance,
  We worshipped at the ancient shrines:
For us the creads joined their dance
  At even in the moonlit pines.

What darkling spell has rent thy skies
  And turned thy heart to steel and fire,
And drawn across thy starry eyes
  The curtains of a wild desire?

THE SPIRIT OF ART

I change not. I am old as Time
  And younger than the dews of morn.
These lips will sing the world's high prime
  Which blessed the toils when life was born.

I am the priestess of the flame
  Which on the eternal alter springs;
Beauty and truth and joy and fame
  Sleep in the shelter of my wings.

I wear the mask of age and clime,
  But he who of my love is fain
Must learn my heart which knows not time,
  And seek my path which fears not pain, —

Till, bruised and worn with wandering
  In the dark wilds my feet have trod,
He hears the songs the Immortals sing
  At even in the glades of God.

Youth

Angel, that heart I seek to know,
　　I fain would make thy word my stay,
Upon thy path I yearn to go
　　If thy clear eyes will light the way.

But ancient loves my memory hold,
　　And I am weak and thou art strong;
I fear the blasts of mountain cold, —
　　Say if the way be dark and long.

The Spirit of Art

On mountain lawns, in meads of spring,
　　With idle boys bedeck thy hair,
Or in deep greenwood loitering
　　Tell to thy heart the world is fair.

That joy I give, but frail and poor
　　Is such a boon, for youth must die;
A little day the flowers endure,
　　And clouds o'erride the April sky.

Upon the windy ways of life,
　　In dark abyss of toil and wrong,
Through storm and sun, through death and strife,
　　I seek the nobler spheral song.

No dulcet lute with golden strings
　　Can hymn the world that is to be.
Out of the jarring soul of things
　　I weave the eternal harmony. —

In forest deeps, in wastes of sand,
　　Where the cold snows outdare the skies:
Where wanderers roam uncharted lands,
　　And the last camp-fire flares and dies:

In sweating mart, in camp and court,
　　Where hopes forlorn have vanquished ease:
Where ships, intent on desperate port,
　　Strain through the quiet of lonely seas:

Where'er o'erborne by sense and sin,
    With bruised head and aching hand,
Guarding the holy fire within,
    Man dares to steel his heart and stand —

Breasting the serried spears of fate,
    Broken and spent, yet joyous still,
Matching against the blind world's hate
    The stark battalions of his will: —

Whoso hath ears, to him shall fall,
    When stars are hid and hopes are dim,
To hear the heavenly voices call,
    And, faint and far, the cosmic hymn —

That hymn of peace when wars are done,
    Of joy which breaks through tears of pain,
Of dawns beyond the westering sun,
    Of skies clear shining after rain.

No sinless Edens know the song,
    No Arcady of youth and light,
But, born amid the glooms of wrong,
    It floats upon the glimmering height,

Where they who faced the dust and scars,
    And shrank not from the fires of hate,
Can walk among the kindred stars,
    Masters of Time and lords of Fate.

And haply then will youth, reborn,
    Restore the world thou fain wouldst hold;
The dawn of an auguster morn
    Will flush thy skies with fairy gold.

The flute of Pan in wildwood glade
    Will pipe its ancient sweet refrain;
Still, still for thee through April shade
    Will Venus and her sister train

Lead the old dance of spring and youth.
    But thine the wiser, clearer eyes,
Which having sought the shrine of truth
    And faced the unending sacrifice,

Can see the myriad ways of man,
    The ecstasy, the fire, the rod,
Of shadows of the timeless plan
    That broods within the mind of God.

Kin to the dust, yet throned on high,
    Thy pride thy bonds, thy bonds release;
Thou see'st the Eternal passing by,
    And in His Will behold'st thy peace.

Processional *(1906)*

Taken from *A Lodge in the Wilderness* (1906), where it is untitled. As 'Processional' it is included in *Poems Scots and English* (1917).

In the ancient orderly places, with a blank and orderly mind,
We sit in our green walled gardens and our corn and oil increase;
Sunset nor dawn can wake us, for the face of the heavens is kind.
We light our taper at even and call our comfort peace.

Peaceful our clear horizon; calm as our sheltered days
Are the lilied meadows we dwell in, the decent highways we tread.
Duly we make our offerings, but we know not the God we praise,
For He is the God of the living, but we, His children, are dead.

I will arise and get me beyond this country of dreams,
Where all is ancient and ordered and hoar with the frost of years,
To the land where loftier mountains cradle their wilder streams,
And the fruitful earth is blessed with more bountiful smiles and tears, —

There in the home of the lightnings, where the fear of the Lord is set
    free,
Where the thunderous midnights fade to the turquoise magic of the
    morn,
The days of man are a vapour, blown from a shoreless sea,
A little cloud before sunrise, a cry in the void forlorn —

I am weary of men and cities and the service of little things,
Where the flamelike glories of life are shrunk to a candle's ray.
Smite me, my God, with Thy presence, blind my eyes with Thy wings,
In the heart of Thy virgin earth show me Thy secret way!

Babylon *(1906)*

This first appeared in Buchan's collection of short stories *The Moon Endureth* (1912).

(The Song of Nehemiah's Workmen)

How many miles to Babylon?
  Three score and ten.
Can I get there by candle-light?
  Yes, and back again.

We are come back from Babylon,
  Out of the plains and the glare,
To the little hills of our own country
  And the sting of our kindred air;
To the rickle of stones on the red rock's edge
  Which Kedron cleaves like a sword.
We will build the walls of Zion again,
  To the glory of Zion's Lord.

Now is no more of dalliance
  By the reedy waters in spring,
When we sang of home, and sighed, and dreamed,
  And wept on remembering.
Now we are back in our ancient hills
  Out of the plains and the sun;

But before we make it a dwelling-place
   There's a wonderful lot to be done.

The walls are to build from west to east,
   From Gihon to Olivet,
Waters to lead and wells to clear,
   And the garden furrows to set.
From the Sheep Gate to the Fish Gate
   Is a welter of mire and mess;
And southward over the common lands
   Is a dragon's wilderness.

The Courts of the Lord are a heap of dust
   Where the hill winds whistle and race,
And the noble pillars of God His House
   Stand in a ruined place.
In the Holy of Holies foxes lair,
   And owls and night-birds build.
There's a deal to do ere we patch it anew
   As our father Solomon willed.

Now is the day of the ordered life
   And the law which all obey.
We toil by rote and speak by note
   And never a soul dare stray.
Ever among us a lean old man
   Keepeth his watch and ward,
Crying, "The Lord hath set you free:
   Prepare ye the way of the Lord."

A goodly task we are called unto,
   A task to dream on o' nights, —
Work for Judah and Judah's God,
   Setting our land to rights;
Everything fair and all things square
   And straight as a plummet string. —
Is it mortal guile, if once in a while
   Our thoughts go wandering? . . .

We were not slaves in Babylon,
    For the gate of our souls lay free,
There in that vast and sunlit land
    On the edges of mystery.
Daily we wrought and daily we thought,
    And we chafed not at rod and power,
For Sinim, Sabaea, and dusky Hind
    Talked to us hour by hour.

The man who lives in Babylon
    May poorly sup and fare,
But loves and lures from the ends of the earth
    Beckon him everywhere.
Next year he too may have sailed strange seas
    And conquered a diadem;
For kings are as common in Babylon
    As crows in Bethlehem.

Here we are bound to the common round
    In a land which knows not change.
Nothing befalleth to stir the blood
    Or quicken the heart to range;
Never a hope that we cannot plumb
    Or a stranger visage in sight, —
At the most a sleek Samaritan
    Or a ragged Amorite.

Here we are sober and staid of soul,
    Working beneath the law,
Settled amid our fathers' dust,
    Seeing the hills they saw.
All things fixed and determinate,
    Chiseled and squared by rule; —
Is it mortal guile once in a while
    To try and escape from school?

We will go back to Babylon,
    Silently one by one,
Out from the hills and the laggard brooks
    To the streams that brim in the sun.

Only a moment, Lord, we crave,
  To breath and listen and see. —
Then we start anew with muscle and thew
  To hammer trestles for Thee.

The Herd of Farawa   *(1907)*

This first appeared in *Am Bolg Solair* (1907) and later in Buchan's own collection *Poems Scots and English* (1917). Buchan introduces the poem 'Who in an April hailstorm discoursed to the traveller on the present discontents. — *Pastorum et solis exegit montibus aevum.-Virgil'*.

Losh, man! Did ever mortal see
        Sic blasts o' snaw? Ye'll bide a wee.
Afore ye think to cross the lea,
        And mount the slack!
Kin'le your pipe, and straucht your knee,
        And gie's your crack!

Hoo lang, ye spier! An unco while!
It's seeventy-sax 'ear came Aprile
That I came frae Auchentyle —
        A bairn o' nine;
And mony's the dreich and dreary mile
        I've gaed sin' syne.

My folk were herds, sae roond the fauld
Afore I was twae towmonts auld
They fand me snowkin', crouse and bauld
        In snaw and seep —
As Dauvid was to kingdoms called,
        Sae I to sheep.

I herdit first on Etterick side.
Dod, man, I mind the stound o' pride
Gaed through my hert, when near and wide
        My dowgs I ran.

Though no seeventeen till Lammastide
        I walked a man.

I got a wife frae Eskdalemuir,
O' dacent herdin' folk, and sair
We wrocht for lang, baith late and 'ear,
        For weans cam fast,
And we were never aucht but puir
        Frae first to last

Tales I could tell would gaur ye grue
O' snawy lambin's warstled through,
O' drifty days, and win's that blew
        Frae norlan' sky,
And spates thet filled the haughlands fou
        And drooned the kye.

But, still and on, the life was fine,
For yon were happier days langsyne;
For gear to hain, and gear to tine
        I had nae care —
Content I was wi' what was mine,
        And blithe to share.

Sic flocks ye'll never see the day,
Nae fauncy ills to mak ye wae,
Nae fauncy dips wi' stawsome broo,
        Wad fricht the French;
We wrocht alang the auld guid way,
        And fand it stench.

Nae mawkit kets, nae scabbit een,
But ilka yowe as trig's a preen;
Sic massy tups as ne'er were seen
        Sin' Job's allowance,
And lambs as thick on ilka green
        As simmer gowans.

Whaur noo ae hirsel jimp can bide
Three hirsels were the countra's pride,
And mony a yaird was wavin' wide,
        And floo'rs were hingin',

Whaur noo is but the bare hillside,
       And linties singin'.
   .   .   .   .   .

And God! the men! Whaur could ye find
Sic hertsome lads, sae crouse and kind;
Sic skeel o' sheep, sic sarious mind
       At kirk and prayer —
Yet aiblins no to haud or bind
       At Boswells fair?

Frae Galloway to Aiberdeen
(I mind the days as 'twere yestreen)
I've had my cantrips — Lord a wheen!
       But through them a',
The fear o' God afore my een,
       I keep't the Law.

My nieves weel hoddit in my breeks,
The Law I keep't, and turned baith cheeks
Until the smiter, saft and meek's
       A bairn at schule;
Syne struck, and laid him bye for weeks
       To learn the fule.

Frae Melrose Cauld to Linkumdoddie,
I'd fecht and drink wi' ony body;
Was there a couthy lad? then, dod, he
       Sune fand his fellow,
What time the tippenny or the toddy
       Had garred us mellow.

Nae wark or ploy e'er saw me shirk;
I had an airm wad fell a stirk;
I traivelled ten lang mile to kirk
       In wind and snaw;
I tell 'e, sir, frae morn to mirk,
       I keep't the Law.
   .   .   .   .   .

Weekly we gat, and never fail,
Screeds marrowy as a pat o' kail,
And awfu' as the Grey Meer's Tail

In Lammas rain,
And stey and lang as Moffatdale,
And stieve's a stane.

Nae Gospel sowens fit for weans,
But doctrines teuch as channel-stanes;
We heard the word wi' anxious pains,
Sarious and happy.
And half the week we piked the banes,
And fand them sappy.

Lang years aneath a man o' God
I sat, my bible on the brod;
He wasna feared to lift the rod
And scaud the errin';
He walked whaur our great forbears trod,
And blest his fairin'.

But noo we've got a bairnly breed,
Whase wee-bit shilpit greetin' screed
Soughs like a wast wind ower the heid,
Lichter than 'oo';
Lassies and weans, it suits their need,
No me and you!

My dochter's servin' in the toun,
She gangs to hear a glaikit loon,
Whae rows his een, and twirls him roun'
Like ane dementit.
Nae word o' Hell, nae sicht or soun'
O' sin repentit.

But juist a weary, yammerin' phrase
O' "Saunts" and "Heaven" and "love" and
"praise,"
Words that a grown man sudna use
God! sic a scunner!
I had to rise and gang my ways
To haud my denner.

At halesome fauts they lift their han',
Henceforth, they cry, this new comman',

Bide quate and doucely in the lan'
        And love your brither —
This is the total end o' man,
        This and nae ither.

And that's their creed! an owercome braw
For folks that kenna fear or fa',
Crouse birds that on their midden craw
        Nor think o' scaith,
That keep the trimmin' o' the Law
        And scorn the pith.

It's no for men that nicht and day
See the Almichty's awesome way,
And ken themselves but ripps o' strae
        Afore His wind,
And, dark or licht, maun watch and pray
        His grace to find.

My forbear, hunkerin' in a hag,
Was martyred by the laird o' Lagg;
He dee'd afore his heid wad wag
        In God's denial.
D'ye think the folk that rant and brag
        Wad thole yon trial?

Man, whiles I'd like to gang mysel
And wile auld Claverse back frae Hell;
Claverse, or maybe Tam Dalziel,
        Wad stop their fleechin';
I wager yon's the lads to mell
        And mend sic preachin'.

Whaure'er I look I find the same,
The warld's nae gumption in its wame;
E'en sin' I mind the human frame
        Grows scrimp and shauchled,
O' a' man's warks ye canna name
        Ane that's no bauchled.

There's mawkit sheep and feckless herds,
And poopits fou o' senseless words;
Instead o' kail we sup on curds,
            And wersh the taste o't;
To parritch-sticks we've turned our swirds,
            Sae mak' the maist o't.

And poalitics! I've seen the day
I'd walk ten mile ower burn and brae
To hear some billie hae his say
            Aboot the nation.
Tories and a' their daft-like play
            Fand quick damnation.

I thought — for I was young — that folk
Were a' the same; I scorned the yoke
O' cless or gear; wi' pigs in poke
            I took nae han'.
I daured the hale wide warld to choke
            The richts o' man.

It's still my creed, but hech! sin' then
We've got the richts and lost the men;
We've got a walth o' gear to spen'
            And nane to spend it;
The warld is waitin' ripe to men',
            And nane to mend it.

Our maisters are a flock o' daws,
Led on by twae-three hoodie craws;
They weir our siller, mak' our laws,
            And God! sic makin'!
And we sit roun' wi' lood applause,
            And cheer their crakin'.

We're great; but daur we lift a nieve
Wi' oot our neebors grant their leave?
We're free, folk say, to speak, believe,
            Dae what we wull —
And what's oor gain? A din to deave
            A yearlin' bull!

.   .   .   .   .   .

A dwaibly warld! I'll no deny
There's orra blessin's. I can buy
My baccy cheap, and feed as high
        For half the siller;
For saxpence ony man can lie
        As fou's the miller.

A bawbee buys a walth o' prent,
And every gowk's in Paurliament;
The warld's reformed — but sir, tak tent,
        For a' their threep,
There's twae things noo that arena kent —
        That's MEN and SHEEP.

To Lionel Phillips   *(1909)*

Lionel Phillips was a colleague of Buchans in South Africa and in 1907 lent his house,
Tylney Hall in Hampshire, for the first night of Buchan's honeymoon. This poem is the
dedication in *Prester John* (1909). It also appears in *Poems Scots and English* (1917).

Time, they say, must the best of us capture,
    And travel and battle and gems and gold
No more can kindle the ancient rapture,
    For even the youngest of hearts grows old.
But in you, I think, the boy is not over;
    So take this medley of ways and wars
As a gift of a friend and a fellow-lover
    Of the fairest country under the stars.

Avignon (1759) *(1909)*

Buchan included the poem in *The Moon Endureth* (1912) and it subsequently appeared in *Poems Scots and English* (1917), *A St Andrews Treasury of Scottish Verse* (1920) and *The Clearing House* (1946).

> *Hearts to break but nane to sell,*
>   *Gear to tine but nane to hain; —*
> *We maun dree a weary spell*
>   *Ere our lad comes back again.*

I walk abroad on winter days,
  When storms have stripped the wide champaign,
For northern winds have norland ways,
  And scents of Badenoch haunt the rain.
And by the lipping river path,
  When in the fog the Rhone runs grey,
I see the heather of the strath,
  And watch the salmon leap in Spey.

The hills are feathered with young trees, —
  I set them for my children's boys.
I made a garden deep in ease,
  A pleasance for my lady's joys.
Strangers have heired them. Long ago
  She died, — Kind fortune thus to die;
And my one son by Beauly flow
  Gave up the soul that could not lie.

Old, elbow-worn, and pinched I bide
  The final toll the gods may take.
The laggard years have quenched my pride;
  They cannot kill the ache, the ache.
Weep not the dead, for they have sleep
  Who lie at home; but ah, for me
In the deep grave my heart will weep
  With longing for my lost countrie.

> *Hearts to break but nane to sell,*
>   *Gear to tine but nane to hain; —*
> *We maun dree a weary spell*
>   *Ere our lad comes back again.*

Wood Magic *(1910)*
(9th Century)

Originally published in *The Moon Endureth* (1912), it has appeared in several anthologies including *Northern Numbers, Second Series* (1921), *Pattern Poetry, Part II* (1926) and *The Scots Weekend* (1936). It is one of the poems in *Poems Scots and English* (1917).

I will walk warily in the wise woods on the fringes of eventide,
    For the covert is full of noises and the stir of nameless things.
I have seen in the dusk of the beeches the shapes of the lords that ride,
    And down in the marish hollow I have heard the lady who sings.
And once in an April gloaming I met a maid on the sward,
    All marble-white and gleaming and tender and wild of eye; —
I, Jehan the hunter, who speak am a grown man, middling hard,
    But I dreamt a month of the maid, and wept I knew not why.

Down by the edge of the firs, in a coppice of heath and vine,
    Is an old moss-grown alter, shaded by briar and bloom,
Denys, the priest, hath told me 'twas the lord Apollo's shrine
    In the days ere Christ came down from God to the Virgin's womb.
I never go past but I doff my cap and avert my eyes —
    (Were Denys to catch me I trow I'd do penance for half a year) —
For once I saw a flame there and the smoke of a sacrifice,
    And a voice spake out of the thicket that froze my soul with fear.

Wherefore to God the Father, the Son, and the Holy Ghost,
    Mary the Blessed Mother, and the kindly Saints as well,
I will give glory and praise, and them I cherish the most,
    For they have the keys of Heaven, and save the soul from Hell.
But likewise I will spare for the lord Apollo a grace,
    And bow for the lady Venus — as a friend and not as a thrall.
'Tis true they are out of Heaven, but some day they may win the place;
    For Gods are kittle cattle, and a wise man honours them all.

An Echo of Meleager   *(1910)*

Published first in *Odd Volume, Vol. 3* (1910) it appears in *Poems Scots and English* (1917) and *The Clearing House* (1946). There are some minor differences in the later versions of the poem.

Scorn not my love, proud child. The summers wane.
　　Long ere the topmost mountain snows have gone
The Spring is fleeting; 'neath the April rain
　　For one brief day flowers laugh on Helicon.
The winds that fan thy honeyed cheek this noon
　　To-morrow will be blasts that scourge the main;
And youth and joy and laughter pass too soon. —
　　Scorn not my love, proud child. The summers wane.

To-day the rose blooms in the garden-plot,
　　The swallows nestle by the Parian dome,
But soon the roses fade and lie forgot
　　And soon the swallows will be turning home.
Tempt not the arrows of the Cyprian's eye,
　　List to the God who will not brook disdain.
Love is the port to which the wise barks fly.
　　Scorn not my love, proud child. The summers wane.

Atta's Song   *(1910)*

Another poem included in *The Moon Endureth* (1912), it has appeared in the anthology *Rosemary* (1920), alongside contributions from G.K. Chesterton, Walter De La Mare, John Galsworthy, Arthur Conan Doyle and Arnold Bennett and in the 1936 edition of *Poems Scots and English.*

I will sing of thee,
Great Sea-Mother,
Whose white arms gather
Thy sons in the ending:
And draw them homeward
From far sad marches —

Wild lands in the sunset,
Bitter shores of the morning —
Soothe them and guide them
By shining pathways
Homeward to thee.

All day I have striven in dark glens
With parched throat and dim eyes,
Where the red crags choke the stream
And dank thickets hide the spear.
I have spilled the blood of my foes,
But their wolves have torn my flanks.
I am faint, O Mother,
Faint and aweary
I have longed for thy cool winds
And thy kind grey eyes
And thy lover's arms.

At the even I came
To a land of terrors,
Of hot swamps where the feet mired
And streams that flowered red with blood.
There I strove with thousands,
Wild-eyed and lost,
As a lion among serpents.
 — But sudden before me
I saw the flash
Of the sweet wide waters
That wash my homeland
And mirror the stars of home.
Then sang I for joy,
For I knew the Preserver,
Thee, the Uniter,
The great Sea-Mother.
Soon will the sweet light come,
And the salt winds and the tides
Will bear me home.

Far in the sunrise,
Nestled in thy bosom,

Lies my own green isle.
Thither wilt thou bear me
To where, above the sea-cliffs,
Stretch mild meadows, flower-decked, thyme-scented,
Crisp with sea breezes.
There my flocks feed
On sunny uplands,
Looking over the waters
To where mount Saos
Raises pure snows to God.

Hermes, guide of souls,
I made thee a shrine in my orchard,
And round thy olive-wood limbs
The maidens twined Spring blossoms —
Violet and helichryse
And the pale wind flowers,
Keep thou watch for me,
For I am coming.
Tell to my lady
And to all my kinsfolk
That I who have gone from them
Tarry not long, but come swift o'er the sea-path.
My feet light with joy,
My eyes bright with longing.
For little it matters
Where a man may fall,
If he fall by the sea-shore;
The kind waters await him,
The white arms are around him,
And the wise Mother of Men
Will carry him home.

I who sing
Wait joyfully on the morning.
Ten thousand beset me
And their spears ache for my heart.
They will crush me and grind me to mire,
So that none will know the man that once was me.
But at the first light I shall be gone,

Singing, flitting, o'er the grey waters,
Outward, homeward,
To thee, the Preserver,
Thee, the Uniter,
Mother the Sea.

Stocks and Stones   *(1911)*

The poem has appeared in The Moon Endureth (1912) *and the 1936 edition of* Poems
Scots and English.

**(The Chief Topiawari replies to Sir Walter Raleigh, who upbraided
him for idol worship.)**

My gods, you say, are idols dumb,
 Which men have wrought from wood or clay,
Carven with chisel, shaped with thumb,
 A mornings task, an evening's play.
You bid me turn my face on high
 Where the blue heaven the sun enthrones,
And serve a viewless deity,
 Nor make my bow to stocks and stones.

My lord, I am not skilled in wit
 Nor wise in priestcraft, but I know
That fear to man is spur and bit
 To jog and curb his fancies' flow.
He fears and loves, for love and awe
 In mortal souls may well unite
To fashion forth the perfect law
 Where Duty takes to wife Delight.

But on each man *one* Fear awaits
 And chills his marrow like the dead. —
He cannot worship what he hates
 Or make a god of naked Dread.

97

The homeless winds that twist and race,
   The heights of cloud that veer and roll,
The unplumb'd Abyss, the drift of Space —
   These are the fears that drain the soul.

Ye dauntless ones from out the sea
   Fear nought. Perchance your gods are strong
To rule the air where grim things be,
   And quell the deeps with all their throng.
For me, I dread not fire nor steel,
   Nor aught that walks in open light,
But fend me from the endless Wheel,
   The voids of Space, the gulfs of Night.

Wherefore my brittle gods I make
   Of friendly clay and kindly stone, —
Wrought with my hands, to serve or break,
   From crown to toe my work, my own.
My eyes can see, my nose can smell,
   My fingers touch their painted face,
They weave their little homely spell
   To warm me from the cold of Space.

My gods are wrought of common stuff
   For human joys and mortal tears;
Weakly, perchance, yet staunch enough
   To build a barrier 'gainst my fears,
Where, lowly but secure, I wait
   And hear without the strange winds blow. —
I cannot worship what I hate
   Or serve a god I dare not know.

The Wise Years   *(1911)*

Taken from *The Moon Endureth* (1912). It also appears in *Northern Numbers (Second Series* 1921).

(The monk, Lapidarius, in meditation)

I, Lapidarius, priest of the Most High
(Called, ere Christ sought me, John of Dinlay-burn),
Now in this shadowy twilight of my days
Give laud and make confession. Yester-eve
I cast lots in the Scriptures, for 'tis right,
As Austin teaches, thus to question God.
Twofold the answer: first I found the text,
"The hour is nigh," a token clear that soon
I must put off these tattered mortal weeds
And don the immortal raiment of the blest.
The second was the Psalm, that "to the just
Peace shall be granted while the moon endures."
A fitting benediction, quoth my soul;
For I have ever loved the moon and sought
The gentle lore that dwelleth in her beams.

Here, in this moorland cell, long years I strove
To pierce the veil that hideth Heaven from man.
By fasts and vigils I wore thin the robe,
The fleshly robe that clogs the soul; in prayer
I from the body soared among the stars
And held high converse with the cherubim.
I moved in ecstasy, and all the land
Spake of my sainthood; people thronged from far
To gaze upon the man who walked with God.
Ah, little knew they! In my heart I wept,
For God was ever distant. Not with Him
I communed, but with fancies self-begot,
Half of sick brain and half of fevered flesh.
And then one eve — 'twas at the Lammas-tide
When every twilight is a taste of Heaven,
While half-distraught I laboured, sudden came

99

The light that shone on Paul; I caught my breath,
Felt on my forehead the cool hand of God,
And heard His holy accents in my ear:
"Why troublest thou thyself to mount to Me
When I am with thee always? Love My world,
The good green earth I gave for thy joy."
Then through the rushes flowered the rose of eve,
And I went forth into the dewy air,
And made my first communion with God's world.

The robe of flesh wears thin, and with the years
God shines through all things. Time and Death are not
Nor Change, but all endures even as a tree
Bears in its secular trunk the rings of youth.
I walk by the stream and hill, at even and dawn,
In noontide's height, in the first joy of spring,
Through the warm hours of summer, in the ripe
Soft fall of autumn, when the winter's spell
Hath stilled the earth to sleep; and as I go
The dear unseen companions walk with me;
The birds and beasts attend me, and their speech,

Wise as the hills, hath opened mysteries.
I hold high fellowship with souls long dead
And souls unborn, for I am one with life,
One with the earth, and almost one with God.
They name me saint no more. The abbot scowls,
The brethren flee me, and the country folk
Call me the devil's minion. Soon, belike, —
For God may will I reach Him through the fire —
They seek to burn me as a brand of hell.
All men have shunned me, but the children come
Stealthily on a holy day with flowers
Or autumn berries; from the hazel shade
They whisper, "Brother John, come play with us,
And tell us stories of your fairy friends."
They know, whose hearts are pure, that mine is kind,
And erreth not in loving all God gave.
They shall have comfort while the moon endures.

The hour is nigh. Behind the wattled strip
Which screens my pallet, lo! the first grey light
Creeps timorous like a fawn. My limbs are moved
To a strange exaltation . . . Soon the sun
Will steep the moorlands in a holier dawn,
And my thin veil of sense will fade and fall.
I shall be one with Him, and hear His speech
As friend to friend, and see Him face to face.
He findeth God who finds the earth He made. . . .
The Green Glen waits the morning, and I go.

The Shorter Catechism *(1911)*
(Revised Version)

Taken from *The Moon Endureth* (1912). It appears in *Poems Scots and English* (1917)
and also in *The Scots Weekend* (1936).

When I was young and herdit sheep,
    I read auld tales o' Wallace wight;
My heid was fou o' sangs and threip
    O' folk that feared nae mortal might.
But noo I'm auld and weel I ken
    We're made alike o' gowd and mire;
There's saft bits in the stievest men
    The bairnliest's got a spunk o' fire.

        Sae hearken to me, lads,
            It's truith that I tell; —
        There's nae man a' courage —
            I ken by mysel'.

I've been an elder forty year,
    I've tried to keep the narrow way,
I've walked afore the Lord in fear,
    I've never missed the kirk a day
I've read the Bible in and oot,
    I ken the feck o't clean by hert; —

101

But still and on I sair misdoot
  I'm better noo than at the stert.

  Sae hearken to me, lads,
    It's truith I maintain! —
  Man's works are but rags, for
    I ken by my ain.

I hae a name for dacent trade;
  I'll wager a' the countryside
Wad swear nae trustier man was made
  The ford to soom, the bent to bide.
But when it comes to coupin' horse
  I'm just like a' that e're were born,
I fling my heels and tak my course —
  I'd sell the minister in the morn.

  Sae hearken to me, lads,
    It's truith that I tell: —
  There's nae man deid honest —
    I ken by mysel'.

Sir Walter Raleigh   *(1911)*

In his book of this title John Buchan notes that when the King reprieved Sir Walter
Raleigh there was great rejoicing and Captain Luttrell declared 'he was in a mood for
singing':

  "The Almiranty of Santa Fee
  Guards to 'tend him had fifty-three;
  And pikes and muskets a goodly store,
  And long-nosed cannons, forty and more
  And five great ships that tossed on the sea,
  Had the Almiranty of Santa Fee.

  Dickon of Devon had nought to his name
  But a ragged shirt and an empty fame,

An old plumed hat and the Devil's own pride,
And a worn old blade that swung at his side.
But he hated Spaniards terribillee, —
And the Almiranty of Santa Fee.

The Almiranty of Santa Fee
Had a laughing lady, fair and free,
Gold in chest and wine in keg,
And pearls as big as a pigeon's egg;
And crosses and jewels so rare to see,
Had the Almiranty of Santa Fee.

Now Dickon came in with the wind, came he,
And burned the castle of Santa Fee,
Slew the guards and rifled the chests,
And tossed the guns to the sea-birds' nests;
And he said to the dame, "Will ye come with me,
Or bide in the ashes of Santa Fee?"

Then up and spoke the lady free,
"It's out of this prison I fain would be.
For I am of England, bred and born,
And I hold all yellow-faced Dons in scorn." —
"Oh, a widowed man this day I be!"
Quo' the Almiranty of Santa Fee."

103

Fratri Dilectissimo   *(1912)*

Taken from *The Marquis of Montrose* (1913). It also appears in *Poems Scots and English* (1917), in *Northern Numbers* (1920), and in a later publication entitled *Montrose* (1928). It was chosen for *Other Men's Flowers* by Field Marshall Viscount A.P. Wavell (1944), *The Clearing House* (1946) by Susan Buchan and for *Buchan Book 2* (1994).

The poem is dedicated to W.H.B., John Buchan's brother Willie, who died at the age of thirty-two in November 1912 when home on leave from the Indian Civil Service.

W.H.B.

When we were little wandering boys,
    And every hill was blue and high,
On ballad ways and martial joys
    We fed our fancies, you and I.
With Bruce we crouched in bracken shade,
    With Douglas charged the Paynim foes;
And oft in moorland noons I played
    Colkitto to your grave Montrose.

The obliterating seasons flow —
    They cannot kill our boyish game.
Though creeds may change and kings may go,
    Yet burns undimmed the ancient flame.
While young men in their pride make haste
    The wrong to right, the bond to free,
And plant a garden in the waste,
    Still rides our Scottish chivalry.

Another end had held your dream —
    To die fulfilled of hope and might,
To pass in one swift rapturous gleam
    From mortal to immortal light —
But through long hours of labouring breath
    You watched the world grow small and far,
And met the constant eyes of Death
    And haply knew how kind they are.

One boon the Fates relenting gave —
    Not where the scented hill-wind blows
From cedar thickets lies your grave,

Nor 'mid the steep Himalayan snows.
Night calls the stragglers to the nest,
    And at long last 'tis home indeed
For your far-wandering feet to rest
    Forever by the crooks of Tweed.

In perfect honour, perfect truth,
    And gentleness to all mankind,
You trod the golden paths of youth,
    Then left the world and youth behind.
Ah no! 'Tis we who fade and fail —
    And you from Time's slow torments free
Shall pass from strength to strength and scale
    The steeps of immortality.

Dear heart, in that serener air,
    If blessed souls may backward gaze,
Some slender nook of memory spare
    For our old happy moorland days.
I sit alone, and musing fills
    My breast with pain that shall not die,
Till once again o'er greener hills
    We ride together, you and I.

In Peebles Churchyard   *(1912)*

Taken from a privately printed book, entitled *John Buchan (1847–1911)*. It was pre-
pared by Anna and John Buchan from the works of their father, his essays, sermons and
poetry. There is an introduction by Anna and the following poem by John Buchan. The
poem was reprinted in the 1936 edition of *Poems Scots and English* (entitled 'To My
Father').

Here by the Tower the mossy headstones lean,
Circled with haggard elms, and the pale sun
With mists begarmented moves down the steep
To wet the wintry even; day is done.
And I am left alone with those who sleep

Beneath the turf still green,
And the dear dust of him who asked no more
Than that his rest in such a shade might be,
Lulled by the river murmering on its shore,
And girdled by the hills' eternity.

Not unattended sleeps he, for around
His kinsfolk keep their ageless company —
Mother and Father and that generous heart
Who dying left an ache that cannot die:
Whose ardour lit the world, and seemed a part
        Of this song-haunted ground.
Ah, lost too soon! how trivial life had grown
When those kind eyes were dimmed, that ardent gaze!
A brother comes; no more thou sleepst alone:
Comrades again as in old boyish days.

The twilight thickens. Now the mountain lines
Dislimn in night; below, from crooked street,
The lights of hearth and casement ope their eyes,
The homeward summons to the wandering feet.
All home in the evening, all save him who lies
        Where never firelight shines.
He sleeps companioned by the fitful stars,
The lone hill winds their ancient comforts bring,
And the white moon peeps through her cloudy bars,
And the wild birds sweep o'er him whispering.

There is no sorrow in so quiet a home:
He hath returned to his own kindly earth.
To him the Mighty Mother gave the key
That wins the riches of her toil and mirth —
The tranced ear to list, the eye to see.
        It was his joy to roam,
In March's pride, in the long July days,
By windy hill, at even and at morn,
And learn the secret of the mystic ways
That God hath walked ere the first dawn was born.

For as an islander in city's glare
Bears in his ear the sound of surf and sea,
And hears the tern call o'er the noisy throng,
So cherished he his happy mystery.
In the dull round of toil his heart was strong,
        Lit by the vision fair.
Ever the cool winds blew upon his face,
The smoke and squalor vanished, and his eyes
Found on his own green hills a resting-place,
And saw St Mary's mirror the calm skies.

He loved all changes that the seasons bring;
Enough for him the homely natural joys;
The wayside flower, the heath-clad mountain rift,
The ferny woodland, were his favoured choice.
Each year with grateful heart he hailed the gift,
        The princely gift of Spring.
Not as the thankless world that takes God's boon
With blinded soul on trivial cares intent,
To him heaven shone in every summer noon,
And every morning was a sacrament.

He loved old ways. The paths of lost romance
Beckoned his steps from many a misty glen.
The long-forgotten voices filled his ear
Of kings now dust and their tall mail-clad men.
Old rimes and pastoral tales to him were dear;
        He saw the Good Folk dance.
For, as the sun ennobles and makes rare
Even common things, so in the gentle ray
Of his clear soul all the wide earth was fair,
And pallid morrows brightened to mid-day.

And yet his lot was hard and drear and strait,
Doing the King's work through the unfeatured years.
He tasted deep of sorrow; loss and death
Brought to his table their full cup of tears.
He knew the ingratitude and envy's breath
        And men's unthinking hate.
They touched him little; when the sun is high

Ill-omened fogs and vapours shrink and cease;
The aches and frailties of mortality
Dissolved in the great noontide of his peace.

That did not come from Nature. She can soothe
And charm her lover, but her spell is brief.
Hers is the opiate, but she knows no cure
For the contagion of our mortal grief.
Not hers to heal the maimed, the foul make pure,
        And the hard high-way smoothe.
For her the young, the joyful, and the strong;
She has no pity for weak souls that crave;
She rules the seasons, gives the birds their song,
And swells the buds — but man she cannot save.

From the deep fountain of Eternal love
He drew his faith that pitieth all mankind,
As some great stream, which eddieth not nor breaks
From its sheer depth and volume. Ever his mind
Was clear and shadowless like mountain lakes
        Where pure skies dream above.
The barren doubts, the little fears that gnaw,
Were solved by deeds and duties, wars to wage
On sin and folly and sorrow. Life he saw
Not as a school but as a pilgrimage.

And, as in Bunyan's tale, he trod the path
From the low lands to the Celestial Town,
No faint-heart Christian, racked with doubts and tears,
Dreading the tempter's lure, the giant's frown,
With his own soul concerned, the sport of fears,
        The cynosure of wrath.
But rather as a Greatheart led the pilgrim band,
Careless of self he toiled to ease the way
For tired limbs, and his strong guiding hand
Made of the desert steeps a holy-day.

He was the Interpreter to untrustful souls;
The weary feet he led into the cool
Soft plain called Ease; he gave the faint to drink;

Dull hearts he brought to the House Beautiful.
The timorous knew his heartening on the brink
       Where the dark River rolls.
He drew men from the town of Vanity
Past Demas' mine and Castle Doubting's towers,
To the green hills where the wise Shepherds be
And Zion's songs are crooned among the flowers.

An endless benediction were his days,
Fulfilled with peace — the glad content of those
Who find a Sabbath stillness in the noise
And in our fevered night the soul's repose;
His were the hidden springs, the secret joys,
       Born of the Holy Place.
From wells of living water streams he drew
To cool the air and wet the parched sod;
And make Heaven's garden, bright with dawn and dew,
For all the haggard world that strives with God.

Honour and praise he asked not; fame i' the sun
Ne'er vexed his thought; nay, even the City of Gold
He would forego if haply, by his loss,
His wearied sheep might safely come to fold.
He was content to hold the world as dross,
       And thereby all things won.
Toiling he found the balm nought mortal yields;
He drew from poverty fullness, joy from pain;
Scattering full-handed, reaped the ample fields;
To him to live was Christ — to die was gain.

Beneath this wintry ground lies many a seed
Hid deep in darkness from the beleaguering air,
Salvage of flowers from autumn's winnowing —
A woeful change from what was once most fair.
But through the nursing earth run fires of spring,
       And in the seasons' need
Dead things will rise to deck the summer's pride,
There wintry prelude past, their birth-pangs o'er,
As the black night prepares for morning-tide,
       And the dim threshold for the radiant door.

Within the porches of immortal joys
He sleeps a little while — a short, brief hour.
Not as this gloaming, harsh with rain and storm,
Closed his life's day; in him the natural power
Was scarce abated, still the blood ran warm —
      His heart a hopeful boy's.
The ford was shallow, and full low the stream,
And happy was the soul that journeyed o'er.
Almost the watchers caught the welcoming gleam,
And saw the Shining Ones that thronged the shore.

Even as some day in the mid-summer's prime
Moves with soft tread from the high thrones of dawn;
In the clear air man goes with lightsome feet;
New hay and clover scent each upland lawn,
Rivers are bright with flags and meadow-sweet,
      The hills a-blow with thyme.
Dusk comes, the woods grow silent, the songs die;
Yet scarce one hour is mute in field and thorn;
For ere the red has left the western sky,
The east is tremulous with the happier morn.

The Eternal Feminine   *(1912)*

Taken from *Poems Scots and English* (1917).

When I was a freckled bit bairn
   And cam in frae my ploys to the fire,
Wi' my buits a' clamjamphried wi' shairn
   And my jaicket a' speldered' wi' mire,
I got gloomin' and glunchin' and paiks,
   And nae bite frae the press or the pan,
And my auld grannie said as she skelped me to bed,
   "Hech, sirs, what a burden is man!"

When I was a lang-leggit lad,
  At waddin's and kirns a gey cheild,

I happit a lass in my maud
And gone cauldrife that she micht hae beild,
  And convoyed her bye bogles and stirks,
A kiss at the hindmost my plan;
  But a' that I fand was the wecht o' her hand,
And "Hech, sirs, what a burden is man!"

When Ailie and me were made yin
  We set up a canty bit cot;
Sair wrocht we day oot and day in,
  We were unco content wi' oor lot.
But whiles wi' a neebor I'd tak
  A gless that my heid couldna' stan';
Syne she'd greet for a week, and nae a word wad she speak
  But "Hech, sirs, what a burden is man!"

She dee'd, and my dochter and me
  For the lave wi' ilk ither maun shift.
Nae tentier lass could ye see;
  The wooers cam doun like a drift;
But sune wi' an unco blae glower
  Frae the doorstep they rade and they ran,
And she'd sigh to hersel', as she gae'd to the well,
  "Hech, sirs, what a burden is man!"

She's mairrit by noo and she's got
  A white-heided lass o' her ain.
White-heided mysel, as I stot
  Roond the doors o' her shouther I'm fain.
What think ye that wean said yestreen?
  I'll tell ye, believe't if ye can;
She primmed up her mou' and said saft as a doo,
  "Hech, sirs, what a burden is man!"

Plain Folk   *(1912)*

First published in *Blackwood's Magazine* in 1912 it was included in *The Moon Endureth* (1912) and the 1936 edition of *Poems Scots and English.*

Since flaming angels drove our sire
From Eden's green to walk the mire,
We are the folk who tilled the plot
And ground the grain and boiled the pot.
We hung the garden terraces
That pleasured Queen Semiramis.
Our toil it was and burdened brain
That set the Pyramids o'er the plain.
We marched from Egypt at God's call
And drilled the ranks and fed them all;
But never Eshcol's wine drank we —
Our bones lay 'twixt the sand and sea.
We officered the brazen bands
That rode the far and desert lands;
We bore the Roman eagles forth
And made great roads from south to north;
White cities flowered for holiday,
But we, forgot, died far away.
And when the Lord called folk to Him,
And some sat blissful at His feet,
Ours was the task the bowl to brim,
For on this earth even saints must eat.

The serfs have little need to think,
Only to work and sleep and drink;
A rover's life is boyish play,
For when cares press he rides away;
The king sits on his ruby throne,
And calls the whole wide world his own.
But we, the plain folk, noon and night
No surcease of our toil we see;
We cannot ease our cares by flight,
For Fortune holds our loves in fee.

112

We are not slaves to sell our wills,
We are not kings to ride the hills,
But patient men who jog and dance
In the dull wake of circumstance;
Loving our little patch of sun,
Too weak our homely dues to shun,
Too nice of conscience, or too free,
To prate of rights — if rights there be.

The scriptures tell us that the meek
The earth shall have to work their will;
It may be they shall find who seek,
When they have topped the last long hill.
Meantime we serve among the dust
For at the best a broken crust,
A word of praise, and now and then
The joy of turning home again.
But freemen still we fall or stand,
We serve because our hearts command.
Though kings may boast and knights cavort,
We broke the spears at Agincourt.
When odds were wild and hopes were down,
We died in droves by Leipsic town.
Never a field was darkly won
But *ours* the dead that faced the sun.
The slave will fight because he must,
The rover for his ire and lust,
The king to pass an idle hour
Or feast his fatted heart with power;
But we, because we choose, we choose,
Nothing to gain and much to loose,
Holding it happier far to die
Than falter in our decency.

The serfs may know an hour of pride
When the high flames of tumult ride.
The rover has his days of ease
When he has sacked his palaces.
A king may live a year like God
When prostrate peoples drape the sod.

We ask for little, — leave to tend
Our modest fields: at daylight's end
The fires of home: a wife's caress:
The star of children's happiness.
Vain hope! 'Tis ours for ever and aye
To do the job the slaves have marred,
To clear the wreckage of the fray,
And please our kings by working hard.
Daily we mend their blunderings,
Swashbucklers, demagogues, and kings!

What if we rose? — If some fine morn,
Unnumbered as the autumn corn,
With all the brains and all the skill
Of stubborn back and steadfast will,
We rose and, with the guns in train,
Proposed to deal the cards again,
And, tired of sitting up 'o nights,
Gave notice to our parasites,
Announcing that in future they
Who paid the piper should call the lay?
Then crowns would tumble down like nuts,
And wastrels hide in water-butts;
Each lamp-post as an epilogue
Would hold a pendent demagogue:
Then would the world be for the wise! —
  .   .   .   .   .   .
But ah! the plain folk never rise.

ॐ   ॐ   ॐ

Thyrsis de nos jours   *(1913)*

An unpublished poem found in the papers of F.S. Oliver, one of Buchan's closest friends and himself an influential writer on imperial affairs. It is but one of several satirical poems Buchan and his circle exchanged during the period. Writing to Buchan on 27 June 1913 Oliver urged his friend to publish the poem for:

> . . . it will just give the finishing tap: the little shove of ridicule which topples the strained edifice. Also it would be a man much bolder than Coeur de Lion or

Crillon who ventured to bring an action for libel on it. Nor do I think it is in fact libellous though I'm not a judge. Not the 'Spectator' I think? What? The Times would be best. I will read it to Robin at Checkenden tomorrow evening.

Attend: I read it to two men who didn't know you at all but are damn good critics like me — of them after a second reading to himself said it was the thing he had been waiting for all his life — the only *fine* modern political rating he'd ever read — The other agreed.

I read it to a solemn meeting of the Round Table Com. last night, they shook their grave sides over it & one & all insisted on publication. Selborne wagged his hands till I thought they would have fallen off.

Yours ever & ever &ever &ever
F.S.O.

Thyrsis, on that tempestuous morn in June
When your brief bright financial bloom seemed o'er,
You filled the welkin with your bootless pleas
And stamped and raved, and all your chamber floor
With bills unpaid and envious summonses
And worthless scrip was strewn.
Friend, I remember yet your parting cry
From the wet platform as you caught your train,
En route for easier lands beyond the main,
The game is up and with the game go I.

Too quick despairer, wherefore didst thou go?
Soon did the high financial pomps come on,
Soon did the pools and corners ripe and swell
To monster gambles in gold-dusted con —
Tango and oil with homely cottage smell
Made stocks a flagrant show.
Noses that down the alleys curve afar
Flock to the spoil, and every week-end sees
Statesmen beneath the dreaming garden trees
Begging their friends to let them in at par.

Alack for Bottomley! three rivals now!
First comes Apella, guardian of the laws;
Next Cleon from the hills, the shepherd-swain
Who pleads with raucous tongue the peoples cause;
And last Thersitas, to whose soothing strain
The nymphs of Progress bow;

They were the first Occasion's hand to seize.
They knew the fruit the earliest tip can yield,
The golden harvest of chequered field,
And what strange crooks are Mammon's tributaries.

An easy access to the hearers' grace
When to the trio Hebrew shepherds sing!
Yet much I fear that envious tales are rife,
True tales that need no fancy's heightening.
Gone is the goal of sad Apella's life,
And Cleon veils his face.
Cleon, ah never more the world will see
Thy Dorian fury on the rich man's scent.
Thy god-like scorn of unearned increment.
For Fate, not Prettyman, has conquered thee.

Thersites of his own will went away.
It urked thee to be here, thou couldst not rest.
To a boon western country thou hast fled,
Unextraditable, rotund, and blest,
Where doubtless now, with flowers engarlanded
In Bacchic holiday,
Thou liest reclined, a Caledonian Shah,
(And purer or more subtle soul than thee
I trow the casual Dago does not see)
Among the septic shades of Bogota.

Too long, too long is now thy absence hence.
Return, my Thyrsis, from thy alien den.
England for thee is now the only home.
And if thou dreadest aught from tongue or pen,
Let in thy ear a whisper often come
To banish all suspense. —
What fearest thou? Resume thine ancient game
New codes, new ethics rule this happier hour.
Doest thou seek proof? Asquith is still in power,
The 'Daily News' still swears by Cleon's fame.

To Sir Reginald Talbot   *(1915)*

Buchan dedicated his historical novel about the Virginia settlers, *Salute to Adventurers*, to his wife Susan's uncle Major-General the Honourable Sir Reginald Talbot, KCB and the dedication appears in the form of the following poem. Talbot had served as an Observer on Sheridan's staff during the American Civil War. The poem appears in *Poems Scots and English* (1917) entitled 'To Sir Reginald Talbot'.

> I tell of old Virginian ways;
>> And who more fit my tale to scan
> Than you, who knew in far-off days
>> The eager horse of Sheridan;
> Who saw the sullen meads of fate,
>> The tattered scrub, the blood-drenched sod,
> Where Lee, the greatest of the great,
>> Bent to the storm of God?
>
> I tell lost tales of savage wars;
>> And you have known the desert sands
> The camp beneath the silver stars,
>> The rush at dawn of Arab bands,
> The fruitless toil, the hopeless dream,
>> The fainting feet, the faltering breath,
> While Gordon by the ancient stream
>> Waited at ease on death.
>
> And now, aloof from camp and field,
>> You spend your sunny autumn hours
> Where the green folds of Chiltern shield
>> The nooks of Thames amid the flowers:
> You who have borne that name of pride,
>> In honour clean from fear or stain,
> Which Talbot won by Henry's side
>> In vanished Aquitaine.

Ordeal by Marriage   *(1915)*
An Eclogue

Ordeal by Marriage, a poetical discussion of aspects of marriage, was privately pub-lished for circulation among John Buchan's friends and is extremely rare. His own copy, passed on to his daughter Alice, was recently sold at Sotheby's. This copy comes from Queen's University, Kingston, Ontario.

The seven characters were all friends of Buchan from Oxford or South Africa. Lionel Curtis would become a distinguished writer on colonial affairs. Philip Kerr was later, as Lord Lothian, British Ambassador to Washington, and Palmedes Zimmern was prob-ably Alfred Zimern, an academic later involved in the League of Nations. Robert Brand, later Lord Brand, had been Buchan's closest friend in South Africa. Lionel Hichens, lat-er Chairman of Cammell Laird, married a cousin of Susan Buchan and Edward Grigg was later Private Secretary to Lloyd George and Lord Altricham.

Susan Buchan later described it as 'a private joke written for a group of friends and quite incomprehensible to anyone else.'

Scene: 23, Cambridge Square, W.

Persons;

Sir Lionel Curtis, *Knight Bachelor*.
Sir Philip Kerr, *Knight Bachelor*.
Sir Palmedes Zimmern, *Knight Bachelor*.
The Hon. Sir Robert Brand, *Knight Bachelor, CMG*.
Major Sir George Craik, *Knight Bachelor*.
Sir Lionel Hichens, *Knight Bachelor*.
Ensign Sir Edward Grigg, *Knight Bachelor (Grenadier Guards)*.

Sir Lionel Curtis. Silence, fair sirs. The Table Round is set.
　　　　　　　　Not since our goodly company first met
　　　　　　　　To weave the silken chain that some day soon
　　　　　　　　Will bind all lands beneath the wandering moon
　　　　　　　　Which hear my Gospel in a *Bundestaat*,
　　　　　　　　Or else a *Staatenbund* – I care not what —
　　　　　　　　But bind at any rate – not since that day
　　　　　　　　Has such a fate-fraught problem come our way,
　　　　　　　　As clouds my soul, makes Philip's visage fall,
　　　　　　　　And Mossie's aspect purely criminal.

　　　　　　　　First, as our wont is, let us briefly quaff
　　　　　　　　The vintage of the copious mimeograph.

Herr Roger Casement writes from Potsdam: —
    "Though
We move by different channels, yet we go
Nobly and sanely to the self-same end,
The doom of England. *Hoch* to you, *mein vriend*!" —
I do not like his tone, but in his soul
There lurks no doubt an image of the Whole.
Sir Harry Britain wires from Medicine Hat: —
"I've often wondered what you all were at.
But your last number's got me fairly hit.
You and Max Aitken are, I reckon, It."
A Mrs Wilkins writes from Wyvenhoe: —
"My dear dead husband loved your paper so.
'Twas while I read it to him yesterday
That his pure spirit gently passed away.
I hope you all will come and see me here;
I have some land and thousands six a year." —
There are five letters, too, from Colney Hatch
Of which the meaning's rather hard to catch.
But all the writers in our praise unite,
And hail us as the Purple Infinite. —

But hence these pleasing flatteries! We must draw
Our mental girdle tight and square our jaw.
The time has come to face a wakening rude
And leave behind our knightly bachelorhood,
Shape to a nobler end our laggard lives,
Seek each a wife – or rather several wives.

I hymn Polygamy – yet not as they,
The swinish crowd who nose the common way.
Divine Philosophy shall be my guide
To lead me to the embraces of my bride,
Or rather brides. – The universe I see
A whirling diverse multiplicity,
Yet through the Various yearning to the Same.
A mighty thinker – I forget his name:
He lived at Moosejaw – put the matter thus:
Anima sola est in omnibus. —
I love his racy *mots*. But mark the point.

We seek the nexus in a world disjoint,
The One our goal. – But not a barren thing,
Not unrelated, sole, uncomforting.
Ah, no! the One in Many is our aim,
Wherein is joined the Different and the Same,
That Unity in Multiplicity
Which holds the young-eyed cherubim in fee.
So for the One the Multiple we need,
As skill equestrian seeks a mettle steed
And no dull farmer's nag. This thought profound
Must guide our conduct in the common round
Of toils and pleasures, and not least in those
Strange ties called love and marriage. Man outgrows
The petty limits of his father's light
And walks unfettered on the starry height.
In wedlock man and wife as one must serve,
So says the Prayer Book. *Unity*, observe.
But at the best a shaveling unity
Starved of its darling multiplicity.
For us I claim a nobler course to run,
Where, free and radiant i' the face o' the sun,
One man and twenty wives shall be as one.
He who would greatly gain must greatly strive
And face with dauntless front full many a wife.
We claim the true fulfilling of the Law,
The loftier ether which the seers foresaw.
Out with base dualism! The One our goal,
Deep, deep in numbers plunge the steadfast soul,
And in the Many find the perfect Whole . . .

So speaks Philosophy. No less strong the case,
For us who seek a true Imperial race,
Which Empire pleads. It is our joy to draw
All creeds and colours to our gentle law,
Kindle their minds, their earnest hearts enthuse,
And set them talking like the very deuce.
But in this godlike task we are not blind
To the old ties and sanctions of mankind.
What stronger chain to lead the world to light
Than numerous wives attached to each Round Table knight?

Conceive the Uplift! To each household's share
A choice selection from the Imperial fair, —
The bold Australian maid from Broken Hill
Whose voice is searching and complexion nil:
The coy New Zealander, the ample Boer,
Of Indian maidens an assorted score:
A shy Tasmanian, one or two Fijis,
And several sirens from the Southern Seas:
And last, to prove that looks are not our thought,
A Hausa lady and a Hottentot.

      .   .   .   .   .   .

Ah, think how strange our moots, how nobly strange,
Where every speech on earth shall freely range!
Ties will we find which Time shall not destroy, —
Make curtain lectures an Imperial joy.

Sir Philip Kerr. Well hath the Prophet spoken. Be it mine
      To proffer water for his ardent wine,
      Such water clear and cool, as erst was seen
      In Castaly's streams and Fountain Hippocrene.
      But not towards Greece adoring eyes I roll,
      For Boston is the Mecca of my soul.
      In this, our hour of need, for help I go
      To Mrs Eddy, first of those who know.
      The truth concealed from seers' and sages' sight
      Is by a Western matron brought to light.

   .   .   .   .   .

      Good is God's world. There is no sting of pain
      In the sweet rose's thorn, no deadly bane
      In the dark nightshade, nor a poisoned gland
      In the lithe snake that leaps to kiss your hand.
      Only the mind of man, corrupt and small,
      Nerveless, inept, of fears a carnival,
      Perverts and clouds the functionings of sense,
      Which but for it were joyous innocence.
      But cleanse the mind and discipline the brain,
      Give to the heart its confidence again,
      And that wise apothegm ye well may know:
      "There is no ill but thinking makes it so."
      To the pure soul a toothache is a sham,
      A stomach-ache not worth a single damn,

Fever, congestion – comforts sent to bless,
A broken limb a call to mirthfulness.

Holding this sanguine creed I must proclaim
Its value on the housetops; sound its fame
From Cliveden to Kamchatka, till the crowd
Of brutish men are at the portent bowed,
And the wide world shall recognise in me
A living proof of its efficiency.
Therefore sweet Pain I woo, and to my heart
I, lover-like, must press the sharpest dart.
And when most men would howl and slap their leg,
I merely smile and cogitate the Egg . . .
Now tell me where in all our mortal round
Such pain, discomfort, misery are found
As in the wedded state? To bow and blench
Before the whimsies of a vapid wench:
To see her face at breakfast, dinner, tea,
And day and night support her ribaldry:
To watch her grow more tiresome day by day
And yet be quite forbid to run away:
To have her tactless humours sprung upon
One's cherished hours of meditation: —
Comely or ugly, well- or under-bred,
It must be simply horrid to be wed.

 .   .   .   .   .   .

And yet to my philosophy this pain,
This ceaseless pain is nothing, but a vain
Vapour which vanishes whene'er the mind
Like a strong sun its mastery can find.
Wherefore I welcome wedlock as a stage
Whereon to prove the truth of Eddy's page.
But not one wife. A myriad is my plea.
Heat the fire seven times that the world may see
How in the torment I my soul will bear
As firm and placid as in Cambridge Square.
Prophet, I will follow thee. Thou ope'st the door,
Set down my name at least for twenty-four.

 .   .   .   .   .

Perchance my arguments may seem too high
To those unversed in Boston's mystery.

Let that Knight speak in whose proud veins there runs
The blood of Zeruiah and Shimei's sons,
Who married copiously ere time began.
I call the Paynim knight, Sir Zimmerman.

Sir Palmedes Zimmern (labouring under deep emotion) sings:

The turtle's voice is in the tree,
    The skies are clear, the rains are gone.
O come, my fair ones, come with me,
    With me, my loves, to Lebanon,
Where 'neath the scented tamarisk boughs
    The cool deep grasses sleep in shade,
And slim young lovers whisper vows,
    Secret and sweet and unafraid.

————————

I am weary to tears of my days among alien races,
    I am sick unto death of this prattle of service and slums,
I detest the toilers (so-called) with their dirty faces,
    And elderly Liberals gnashing their toothless gums.
I simply abominate Blue-books and social communions,
    Smug politicians and earnest young donkeys that try to improve.
Unions I seek, but another sort than Trade Unions,
    Henceforth my life I devote to the questing of love.

————————

In the years that are glorious and golden,
    Where Abana sings to the sea,
In a myriad embraces enfolden —
All. Hush!

Sir P. Zimmern. I shall live as the harts on the lee.
    Then kisses shall welcome the noon-tide,
        Soft kisses that shudder and cling,
    And rapture shall waken the moon-tide —
All (very emphatically). Hush!!

Sir P. Zimmern (trying a new metre):
    Foot of fawn in the greenwood
        Shall be less fleet than me.

Wind of morn in the treetops
　　Shall be less free.
Myriad maids shall attend me,
　　And love me well —

Sir G. Craik (speaking with emotion). Hell!

　　(*He goes out and returns sipping a strong whisky-and-soda, to
　　the obvious disapproval of Sir R. Brand.*)

Sir Robert Brand. A Banker I, a member of the house
　　Founded long since by sainted Lazarus,
　　Who made a scoop and piled a goodly hoard
　　Out of crumbs that fell from Dives' board.
　　I love not Eastern fervours nor the sham
　　Gold of the Christian Scientist. I damn
　　All sort of metaphysics, bad or good.
　　They spoil my sleep and put me off my food.
　　Give me hard facts and honest figures — then
　　I can talk plainly as to business men.
　　This problem now before us — I admit
　　Its gravity, and seek to bring to it
　　A sober City judgment, fair and free,
　　And find its answer in the rule of three.

　　　　　　·　　　·　　　·　　　·　　·　　　·

　　At such a moment, so it seems to me,
　　Our single quest must be economy,
　　Else for the war we cannot pay the score
　　Without our credit sinking through the floor.
　　And 'tis by credit, be it understood,
　　My firm doth earn its meagre livelihood.
　　But mark, economy is not more meet
　　For spendthrift blades that house in Downing Street,
　　And rob the public coffers, than for him
　　Who lives in *rentier's* life, or in the dim
　　Twilight of modest earnings, such as Zim.
　　From Balham's humble roof to Chatsworth's dome,
　　Economy must permeate the home.
　　Now ever since old Lot from Sodom's pales
　　Fled to a sanctuary in Edom's vales,

124

Man has had woman hanging to his tails.
Nor, like the patriarch, can he her exalt
Into a pillar of good kitchen salt.
Statistics just compiled by Mr Bangs
Show that around the average neck there hangs
A female millstone — nay, not less than five,
Whom he must house and clothe and keep alive;
Remote and impecunious relatives,
Cousins and aunts and grandmothers and wives,
Cooks, housemaids, scullions, typewriters galore,
And secretaries — Heaven knows how many more.
It is our duty, and we do not shrink,
But at this hour, with England on the brink
Of economic crisis, let's be sure
We guiltless are of vain expenditure.
Each female separate household is a call
And drain upon our dwindling capital,
Which would be remedied if we but got
Under one single rooftree all the lot.
In rates and lighting, breakages and rent,
Each man would save, I reckon, nine per cent.
And since they will not come unless they're wed,
The let us marry 'em, and no more be said.
Simple my plea: Let us forthwith convey
Our females into hotchpot, as they say.
I shall a building presently prepare
In the vicinity of Cambridge Square,
With all amenities of light and air,
Where I propose my various wives to pen,
Fitted for eight, and at a pinch for ten.
They shall be stayed with apples, round and red,
And inexpensive fruits, and Standard Bread.
So shall I aid the general Uplift.
Polygamy, you say: I call it thrift.
And if the Hirsts and Paishes me revile,
I answer, with a slow and secret smile
Like Monna Lisa's: "In this way alone
I can assist the Government with their loan,
And at my country's enemies heave a stone."

Sir Edward Grigg. I'm sorry to look like a prig,
　　　　　But since I a soldier became,
　　　　　My notions have changed with my rig,
　　　　　They could scarcely continue the same.
　　　　　I am all for espousing a dame
　　　　　When I'm weary of battles and swords,
　　　　　But Polygamy is not in the game —
　　　　　It's simply not done in the Guards.

　　　　　It's true that our hearts they are big,
　　　　　That our bosoms are swift to inflame;
　　　　　That our fancies, like birds on a twig,
　　　　　Few maidens are able to tame;
　　　　　That Beauty — for such is our fame —
　　　　　Must yield to our eyes and our words;
　　　　　But Polygamy — oh, no, for shame!
　　　　　It's simply not done in the Guards.

　　　　　Our men sometimes drink like a pig,
　　　　　And their morals are halting and lame;
　　　　　For certain, their views are not Whig,
　　　　　And celibacy is not their aim.
　　　　　There is much that a censor might blame —
　　　　　Wine, women, and horses and cards;
　　　　　But Polygamy — perish the name!
　　　　　It's simply not done in the Guards.

　　　　　　　　Envoi.

　　　　　Dear Prophet, I don't care a fig
　　　　　For your Uplift and future rewards.
　　　　　As a friend I give warning, you twig,
　　　　　It's simply not done in the Guards.

Sir Lionel Hichens. I deprecate the unseemly levity
　　　　Of the last knight as fitter for a free
　　　　And ill-conducted pot-house than for us,
　　　　Whose pride is to be deadly serious.
　　　　Yet with his ill-put thesis I agree;

A suave decorum must our *métier* be,
Standing as exemplar, on my advice,
Of all that is not only good, but nice.

.   .   .   .   .

From a full heart I speak. This very day
I've held three thousand miscreants in play.
The vile mechanic scum by Mersey's waves
Decline alike to Britons be — or slaves.
An addle-pated Government blinks the truth;
Nor succour can I get from George or Booth.
A single workman is a decent soul;
I know his thoughts, and like him on the whole;
But multiply him by a thousand — then
You find you're met by mountebanks, not men.
A crowd's mentality does not represent
An adding of the units component.
In kind 'tis different and 'tis vastly bad;
A man's a gentleman, a mob's a cad.
Wherefore with all the unction I command
I plead for singleness in marriage bond.
Your plural wives will quickly organise
Into a Union with paid secretaries.
No more a little coaxing, a caress,
An opera box, perhaps a Paris dress,
Will mend connubial tiffs. Their Union rules
Will make the best of women act like fools;
Strikes there will be, and endless arguing.
Marriage no more will be a silken string,
But a great hempen cable: one rash word
Will loose upon you an embattled horde.
Ah! how my fancy paints the wretched man
Trimming and truckling to each harridan,
His front door picketed, should he fail to stoop,
And all his comforts fairly in the soup.

.   .   .   .   .

I am a man of deeds, not words. Be led
By my wise counsel. What I have said, I've said.

Sir George Craik (corrugating his forehead).
        Prophet of Prophets, known of old,

127

Master of all who strive and seek,
Beneath whose awful eye we hold
    Our solemn conclaves week by week,
        And con the Imperial alphabet,
        Lest we forget, lest we forget.

The tumult and the shouting die;
    Bob is already fast asleep,
And only Zimmern's eerie cry
    Stirs Philip from his brooding deep.
        Grigg strokes his lip's incipient hair,
        In case it's there, in case it's there.

I'm a policeman, blunt and plain;
    Likewise a soldier and a Scot;
And so I say with might and main,
    What seems to be by all forgot:
        This whole discussion's nought but fun,
        It can't be done, it can't be done.

Your airy projects well may suit
    Some lesser breed without the Law;
Some dusky Polynesian moot,
    Or high-browed youths in Arkansaw.
        But Englishmen are Christians yet,
        So don't forget, so don't forget.

High in our ancient legal brass
    'Tis writ that man may have one mate;
And he who would that rule o'erpass
    Is courting trouble, sure as fate;
        For were he hero, sage, or god,
        He'd go to quod, he'd go to quod.

Now prophets since the world began
    Have had their sorrows and have thriven;
The Senate's curse, the Church's ban,
    Have opened them the gate to Heaven.
        Stonings and scourgings, pain and shame,
        Have helped their fame, have helped their fame.

But there was never prophet born
   Who could appear before the beaks
For bigamy, and bear the scorn
   With which they gave him thirty weeks.
      The loftiest fame these weeks would kill
      In Pentonville, in Pentonville.

Wherefore I bid you cast behind
   Your fantasies of pen and tongue,
And rather fix your roving mind
   On Roosevelt, than on Brigham Young.
      Go home, and after this carouse
      Peruse "The Angel in the House."

(*Confusion reigns.* Sir P. Zimmern *repeats the Song of Solomon in a corner, till he is led away by* Sir Philip Kerr. *One by one the company depart, leaving* Sir Lionel Curtis *gesticulating on the hearth-rug.*)

The South Countrie   *(1916)*

Taken from *Poems Scots and English* (1917). It also appears in *A St Andrews Treasury of Scottish Verse* (1920), *A Book of Scots* (1925), *A Book of Twentieth Century Verse* (1925), and in *Buchan Book 2* (1994).

I never likit the Kingdom o' Fife —
   Its kail's as cauld as its wind and rain,
And the folk that bide benorth o' the Clyde
   They speak a langwidge that's no my ain.
Doun in the west is a clarty nest,
   And the big stane cities are no for me;
Sae I'll buckle my pack on my auld bent back
   And tak the road for the South Countrie.

Whaur sall I enter the Promised Land,
   Ower the Sutra or doun the Lyne,
Up the side o' the water o' Clyde

Or cross the muirs at the heid o' Tyne,
Or staucherin' on by Crawfordjohn
   Yont to the glens whaur Tweed rins wee? —
It's maitter sma' whaur your road may fa'
   Gin it land ye safe in the South Countrie.

You are the hills that my hert kens weel,
   Hame for the weary, rest for the auld,
Braid and high as the Aprile sky,
   Blue on the taps and green i' the fauld:
At ilka turn a bit wanderin' burn,
   And a canty biggin' on ilka lea —
There's nocht sae braw in the wide world's schaw
   As the heughs and holms o' the South Countrie.

You are the lads that my hert loes weel,
   Frank and couthy and kind to a',
Wi' the open broo and the mirthfu' mou'
   And the open door at the e'enin's fa';
A trig hamesteid and a lauchin' breed
   O' weans that hearten the auld to see —
Sma' or great, can ye find the mate
   O' the folk that bide in the South Countrie?

The lichtist fit that traivels the roads
   Maun lag and drag as the end grows near;
Threescore and ten are the years o' men,
   And I'm bye the bit by a lang lang year.
Sae I'll seek my rest in the land loe'd best,
   And ask nae mair than that God shall gie
To my failin' een for the hinmost scene
   The gentle hills o' the South Countrie.

The Kirn[1] *(Idyll vii)*   *(1916)*

Taken from *Poems Scots and English* (1917), from the section entitled *Theocritus in Scots*. An extract, 'Jock's Song' appears in *A Scots Garland* (1931).

'Twas last back-end that me and Dauvit Sma'
And Robert Todd, the herd at Meldonha',
The hairst weel ower and under rape and thack,
Set oot to keep the kirn at Haytounslack,
Wat Laidlaw's fairm — for Wat's the rale stench breed
The borders kenned afore the auld lairds dee'd,
And a' the soor-milk Wast ran doun the Tweed.

We werna half the road, nor bye the grain
Whaur auncient Druids left the standin' stane,
When Gidden Scott cam heinchin' ower the muir,
Gidden the wale o' men; ilk kirn and fair,
Clippen' and spainin', was a cheerier place
For ae sicht o' his honest bawsened face.
He was a drover, famed frae Clyde to Spey,
The graundest juidge o' beasts — a dealer tae.
His furthy coat o' tup's 'oo spun at hame,
His weel-worn maud that buckled roond his wame,
His snootit kep that hid the broos aneath,
His buits wi' tackets like a harrow's teeth,
His shairny leggin's and his michty staff
Proclaimed him for a drover three mile aff.

"Losh! lads," he cried, "whaur are traivellin' noo,
Trig as the lassies decked for them they loe?
Is't to a countra splore, or to the toun
Whaur creeshy baillies to their feasts sit doun?
Or is't some waddin' wi' its pipes and reels
That gars the chuckies loup ahint your heels?"

"Weel met," says I. "The day our jaunt we mak
To join Wat Laidlaw's kirn at Haystounslack.
Lang is the gait, and, sin' it's pairtly yours,
What say ye to a sang to wile the 'oors?

In a' the land frae Wigtoun to the Mearns
There's nane that ploos sae straucht the rig o' Burns
As your guid sel' (so rins the countra sough);
And I, though frae sic genious far eneuch,
I, tae, hae clinkit rhymes at orra whiles.
We'll niffer sangs to pass the muirland miles."

"Na, Jock," says he, and wagged a sarious pow,
"Sma' share hae I in that divinest lowe.
A roopy craw as weel a pairt micht claim
I' the laverock's sang as me in Robin's fame.
But sin' we're a' guid freends, I'll sing a sang
I made last Monday drovin' ower the Whang."[2]

Gidden's Song

Sin' Andra took the jee and gaed aff across the sea
   I'm as dowff as ony fisher-wife that watches on the sand,
I'm as restless as a staig, me that aince was like a craig,
   When I think upon yon far frem't land.

We had a cuisten oot, I mindna what aboot;
   We had feucht a bit and flytit and gien and taen the blow;
But oor dander was nae mair than the rouk in simmer air,
   For I loe'd him as a lassie loes her joe.

He had sic a couthy way, aye sae canty and sae gay;
   He garred a body's hert loup up and kept the warld gaun roun';
The dreichest saul could see he had sunlicht in his ee,
   And there's no his marrow left in the toun.

We were 'greed like twae stirks that feed amang the birks,
   My every thocht I shared wi' him, his hinmost plack was mine;
We had nocht to hide frae ither, he was mair to me than brither;
   But that's a bye wi't langsyne.

As I gang oot and in, in my heid there rins a tune,
   Some tune o' Andra's playin' in the happy days that's gane.

132

When I sit at festive scene there's a mist comes ower my een
For the kind lad that's left me my lane.

So Gidden spak, and ower the lave o' us cam
A sadness waur than penitential psalm.
The tune was cried; nae jovial rantin' stave
Wad set a mood sae pensive and sae grave.
Sae, followin' on, I cleared my hass and sung
A sang I made langsyne when I was young.

Jock's Song

Sing, lads, and bend the bicker; gloamin' draps
      On Winston side.
A' ye that dwal in sicht o' Tintock's taps
      Frae Tweed to Clyde
Gae stert your reels and ding the warlock Care
      At young bluid's call
The wind that blaws frae yont the mountain muir
      Will steal my saul.

Mind ye the lass that used to bide langsyne
      At Coulter-fit?
(Gae pipe your sprigs, for youth is ill to bin'
      And pleesures flit.)
Her mither keep't the inn, and doun the stair
      A' day wad bawl.
The wind that blaws frae yont the mountain muir
      Will steal my saul.

My heid rins round — I think they ca'd her Jean.
      She looked sae high,
She walked sae prood, it micht hae been the Queen
      As she gaed bye,
Buskit sae trig, and ower her yellow hair
      A denty shawl.
The wind that blaws frae yont the mountain muir
      Will steal my saul.

Ae day the King himsel' was ridin' through
        And saw her face.
He telled his son, "For ae kiss o' her mou
        I'd change my place
Wi' ony gangrel, roup my royal share,
        My kingly hall."
That wind that blaws frae yont the mountain muir
        Will steal my saul.

I kenna if I loe'd the lassie true,
        But this I ken;
To get a welcome frae her een o' blue,
        To see again
Her dimpled cheek, ten 'ears o' life I'd spare
        In prison wall.
The wind that blaws frae yont the mountain muir
        Will steal my saul.

Ae simmer morn when a' the lift was clear
        And saft winds sighed,
Wi' kilted coats I saw her wanderin' near
        The birnie's tide.
Thinks I, Queen Mary was na half as fair
        In days o' aul'.
The wind that blaws frae yont the mountain muir.
        Will steal my saul.

Sing, lads, and bend the bicker; e'enin' fa's —
        My denty doo
Has sell't hersel' for gowd and silken braws
        The weemen loe.
A feckless laird has bocht her beauty rare,
        Her love, her all.
The wind that blaws frae yont the mountain muir
        Will steal my saul.

I watched them as their coach gaed ower the pass
        Wi' blindit een;
A shilpit carle aside the brawest lass
        That Scotland's seen.

Far, far she's gane, and toom the warld and puir
   Whaur I maun dwal.
The wind that blaws frae yont the mountain muir
   Will steal my saul.

A' day I wander like a restless ghaist
   Ower hill and lea;
The gun hangs in the spence, the rod's unused,
   The dowg gangs free.
At nicht I dream, and O! my dreams are sair,
   My hert's in thrall.
The wind that blaws frae yont the mountain muir
   Has stown my saul.

Loud Gidden spak; "Weel dune! — The convoy's ower.
Here we maun pairt, for I'm for Auchenlour.
Oor forebears, when they set a makkers' test
Gied cups and wreaths to him that sang the best.
Nae drink hae I, thae muirland floo'ers are wauf,
Sae tak for awms my trustit hazel staff."

We cried guid-fairin' to his massy back,
And turned intil the road for Haystounslack.
Aroond the hills and heughs the gloamin' crap,
And a braw mune cam ridin' ower the slap.
The stirlin's crooded thick as flees in air,
An auld blackcock was flytin' on the muir.
Afore the steadin' cairts were settin' doun
Ilk snoddit lassie in her kirk-gaun gown,
And bauld young lads were swingin' up the braes,
Ilk ane wi' glancin' een and dancin' taes.
The fiddles scrapit and atower the din
The "Floo'ers o' Embro" soughed oot on the win'.
Furth frae the ben cam sic a noble reek
That hungry folk maun snowk but daurna speak; —
Haggis and tripe, and puddin's black, and yill,
And guid saut beef and braxy frae the hill,
Crisp aiten farles, bannocks and seein' kail;
And at the door stood Wat to cry us hail.
His walie nieves upheld a muckle bowl

Whase spicy scent was unction to the saul.
His ladle plowtered in the reamin' brew,
And for us three he filled the rummers fou.
Nae nectar that the auld gods quaffed on hie,
Nae heather wine wanchancy warlocks prie,
Nae Well o' Bethlehem or Siloam's pule,
Was ever half as guid as Wattie's yill.

Heaven send anither 'ear that I gang back
To drink wi' honest folk at Haystounslack!

Footnotes given in *Poems Scots and English* read as follows:

1 The Greek text has not been followed in the songs, as it would be hard to find equivalents for Lycidas and
Simichidas in Lowland Scots. Jock's song is a free paraphrase of Victor Hugo's 'Guitare'. How close that famous lyric is to the Theocritus manner will be admitted by those who remember Walter Headlam's Greek version
of it.
2 The Lang Whang is the old Edinburgh–Lanark road.

The Fishers (Idyll xxi)   *(1916)*

Taken from *Poems Scots and English* (1917), from the section entitled *Theocritus in
Scots*. It also appears in *An Anglers Garland of Fields, Rivers, and other Country Contentments* (1920), and *The Northern Muse* (1924).

'Tis puirtith sooples heid and hand
And gars inventions fill the land;
And dreams come fast to folk that lie
Wi' nocht atween them and the sky.

Twae collier lads frae near Lasswade,
Auld skeely fishers, fand their bed
Ae simmer's nicht aside the shaw
Whaur Manor rins by Cademuir Law.
Dry flowe-moss made them pillows fine,
And, for a bield to kep the win',
A muckle craig owerhung the burn,

A' thacked wi' blaeberry and fern.
Aside them lay their rods and reels,
Their flee-books and their auncient creels.
The pooches o' their moleskin breeks
Contained unlawfu' things like cleeks,
For folk that fish to fill their wame
Are no fasteedious at the game.

The twae aye took their jaunts thegither;
Geordie was ane and Tam the ither.
Their chaumer was the mune-bricht sky,
The siller stream their lullaby.

When knocks in touns were chappin' three,
Tam woke and rubbed a blinkin' ee.
It was the 'oor when troots are boun'
To gulp the May-flee floatin' doun,
Afore the sun is in the glens
And dim are a' the heughs and dens.

Tam

"Short is the simmer's daurk, they say,
But this ane seemed as lang's the day:
For siccan dreams as passed my sicht
I never saw in Januar' nicht.
If some auld prophet chiel were here
I wad hae curious things to speir."

Geordie

"It's conscience gars the nichtmares rin,
Sae, Tam my lad, what hae ye dune?"

Tam

"Nae ill; my saul is free frae blame,
Nor hae I wrocht ower hard my wame,
For last I fed, as ye maun awn,

On a sma' troot and pease-meal scone.
But hear my dream, for aiblins you
May find a way to riddle't true. . . .

I thocht that I was castin' steady
At the pule's tail ayont the smiddy,
Wi' finest gut and sma'est flee,
For the air was clear and the water wee;
When sudden wi' a roust and swish
I rase a maist enormous fish. . . .
I struck and heuked the monster shure,
Guidsakes! to see him loup in air!
It was nae saumon, na, nor troot;
To the last yaird my line gaed oot,
As up the stream the warlock ran
As wild as Job's Leviathan.
I got him stopped below the linn,
Whaur very near I tummled in,
Aye prayin' hard my heuk wad haud;
And syne he turned a dorty jaud,
Sulkin' far doun amang the stanes.
I tapped the but to stir his banes.
He warsled here and plowtered there,
But still I held him ticht and fair,
The water rinnin' oxter-hie,
The sweat aye drippin' in my ee.
Sae bit by bit I wysed him richt
And broke his stieve and fashious micht,
Till sair fordone he cam to book
And walloped in a shallow crook.
I had nae gad, sae doun my wand
I flang and pinned him on the sand.
I claucht him in baith airms and peched
Ashore — he was a michty wecht;
Nor stopped till I had got him shure
Amang the threshes on the muir.

Then, Geordie lad, my een aye rowed
The beast was made o' solid gowd! —
Sic ferlie as was never kenned,

A' glitterin' gowd frae end to end!
I lauched, I grat, my kep I flang,
I danced a sprig, I sang a sang.
And syne I wished that I micht dee
If wark again was touched by me. . . .

Wi' that I woke; nae fish was there —
Juist the burnside and empty muir.
Noo tell me honest, Geordie lad,
Think ye yon daftlike aith will haud?"

Geordie

"Tuts, Tam ye fule, the aith ye sware
Was like your fish, nae less, nae mair.
For dreams are nocht but simmer rouk,
And him that trusts them hunts the gowk. . . .
It's time we catched some fish o' flesh
Or we will baith gang brekfastless."

Sweet Argos   *(1916)*

Taken from *Poems Scots and English* (1917). It is introduced as 'An Epistle from Jock
in billets to Sandy in the trenches'.

When the Almichty took His hand
  Frae shapin' skies and seas and land,
Some orra bits left ower He fand,
  Riddled them roun' —
A clart o' stane and wud and sand —
  And made this toun.

A glaury loan, a tumblin' kirk,
Twae glandered mears, a dwaibly stirk,
Hens, ae auld wife, a wauflike birk —
  That's whaur I dwal,

While you are fechtin' like a Turk
   Ayont Thiepval.

The weet drips through the bauks abune,
Ootbye the cundies roar and rin,
There's comfort naether oot nor in,
   The wind gangs blather; —
We maun be michty sunk in sin
   To earn sic wather.

But, Sandy lad, for you it's waur,
You on that muckle Zollern scaur,
Your lintwhite locks a' fyled wi' glaur,
   And hungry — my word!
While Gairmans dae the best they daur
   To send you skyward. . . .

  .   .   .   .   .   .

'Twas late yestreen that we cam doun
The road that leads frae Morval toun;
We cam like mice, nae sang nor soun',
   Nae daff nor jest;
Like ghaists that trail the midnicht roun'
   We crap to rest.

For sax weeks hunkerin' in a hole
We'd kenned the warst a man can thole —
Nae skirlin' dash frae goal to goal
   Yellin' like wud,
But the lang stell that wechts the soul
   And tooms the bluid.

Weel, yestreen we limped alang,
Me and auld Dave frae Cambuslang,
And Andra, him that had the gang
   In Tamson's mills,
And Linton Bob that wrocht amang
   The Pentland Hills.

And as we socht oor shauchlin' way
Atween the runts o' Bernafay,

The mune ayont the darkenin' brae
    Lichted a gap.
Bob peched. "Ma God," I heard him say,
    "The Cauldstaneslap!"

Syne we won ower the hinmost rig
Amang the dumps, whaur warm and trig
The braziers lowe and wee trucks jig
    Frae bing to ree.
Dave gripped my airm. "It's fair Coatbrig!"
    He stepped oot free. . . .

   .   .   .   .   .

This morn I'm sittin' on a box,
Reddin' an unco pair o' socks,
Watchin' the yaird whaur muckle docks
    And nettles blaw,
And turks' caps, marygolds and phlox
    Stand in a raw.

The berry busses hing wi' weet,
The smiddy clang comes doun the street,
A coo is routin', bairnies greet,
    A young cock craws. —
I shut my een; my traivelled feet
    Were back i' the Shaws.

Back twenty year. A tautit wean,
I heard my granny's voice complain
O' bursted buits: I saw the rain
    Rin aff the byre;
The burn wi' foamin' yellow mane
    Roared doun the swire.

A can o' worms ae pooch concealed,
The tither scones weel brooned and jeeled;
Let eld sit cowerin' in the beild,
    Youth maun be oot;
The rain may pour, he's for the field
    To catch a troot. . . .

   .   .   .   .   .

And, Sandy lad, a stand o' joy
Gaed through my breist. A halflin's ploy,
An auld wife's tale, a bairnies toy,
   A lassie's favour,
Are things nae war can clean destroy
   Nor kill the savour.

It's in sma' things that greatness lies,
The simple aye confoonds the wise,
The towers that ettle at the skies
   Crack, coup and tummle,
The blather, swalled to unco size,
   Bursts wi' a rummle. . . .

Straucht to the Deil oor hainin's fly;
A spate can droon the best o' kye:
The day oor heids we cairry high
   And wanton rarely: —
The morn in some black sheugh dounbye
   We floonder sairly.

The breist o' man is fortune-pruif
He heeds nor jade nor deil nor cuif,
If twae-three things the Guid Folk give
   His lot to cheer,
The sma' things that oor mortal luve
   Maun aye haud dear.

What gaurs us fecht? It's no the law,
Nor poaliticians in a raw,
Nor hate o' folk we never saw; —
   Oot in yon hell
I've killed a wheen – the job wad staw
   Auld Hornie's sel'.

It's luve, my man, nae less and nae mair, —
Luve o' auld freends at kirk and fair,
Auld-farrant sangs that memories bear
   O' but and ben,
Some wee cot-hoose far up the muir
   Or doun the glen.

And Gairmans are nae doot the same:
The lad ye've stickin' in the wame
Fechts no for deevilment or fame,
    But juist for pride
In his bit dacent canty hame
    By some burnside.

It's queer that the Almichty's plan
Sud set oot man to fecht wi' man
For the same luve — their native lan',
    And wife and weans.
It's queer, but threep the best ye can,
    The truith remains.

The warld's a fecht. Frae star to stane
The hale Creation strives in pain.
Paiks maun be tholed by ilk alane,
    The cup be drainit,
If man's to get the bunemost gain
    That God's ordainit.

But luve's the fire that keeps him gaun,
Ilk puir forjaskit weariet man.
Hate sparks like pouther in the pan,
    And pride will flicker,
But luve will burn till skies are faun,
    Mair clear and siccar.

And a' we socht o' honest worth
We'll find again in nobler birth,
For Heaven itsel' begins on earth,
    And caps the riggin'
O' what in pain and toil and dearth
    We've aye been biggin'.

Nae walth o' gowden streets for me;
I ask but that my een sud see
The auld green hopes, the broomy lea,
    The clear burn's pules,
And wander whaur the wind blaws free
    Frae heather hills.

Sae, Sandy, if it's written true
That you and me sud warstle through,
Wi' whatna joy we'll haud the ploo
    And delve the yaird!
Ten thoosandfauld the mair we'll loe
    Oor Border swaird!

But if like ither dacent men
We've looked oor last on Etterick glen
And some day sune we'll see the en'
    That brings nae shame,
We'll face't, — for in that 'oor we'll ken
    We're hame, we're hame.

On Leave   *(1916)*

Taken from *Poems Scots and English* (1917). It also appears in *The Northern Muse*
(1924), and *Poems of the First World War* (1993).

I had auchteen months o' the war,
    Steel and pouther and reek,
Fitsore, weary and wauf, —
    Syne I got hame for a week.

Daft-like I entered the toun,
    I scarcely kenned for my ain.
I sleepit twae days in my bed,
    The third I buried my wean.

The wife sat greetin' at hame,
    While I wandered oot to the hill,
My hert as cauld as a stane,
    But my heid gaun roond like a mill.

I wasna the man I had been, —
    Juist a gangrel dozin' in fits; —

The pin had faun oot o' the warld,
    And I doddered amang the bits.

I clamb to the Lammerlaw
    And sat me doun on the cairn; —
The best o' my freends were deid,
    And noo I had buried my bairn; —

The stink o' gas in my nose,
    The colour o' bluid in my ee,
And the bidden' o' Hell in my lug
    To curse my Maker and dee.

But up in that gloamin' hour,
    On the heather and thymy sod,
Wi' the sun gaun doun in the Wast
    I made my peace wi' God. . . .

I saw a thoosand hills,
    Green and gowd i' the licht,
Roond and backit like sheep,
    Huddle into the nicht.

But I kenned they werna hills,
    But the same as mounds ye see
Doun by the back o' the line
    Whaur they bury oor lads that dee.

They were juist the same as at Loos
    Whaur we happit Andra and Dave. —
There was naething in life but death,
    And a' the warld was a grave.

A' the hills were graves,
    The graves o' the deid langsyne,
And somewhere oot in the Wast
    Was the grummlin' battle-line.

But up frae the howe o' the glen
    Came the waft o' the simmer een.

The stink gaed oot o' my nose,
  And I sniffed it, caller and clean.

The smell o' the simmer hills,
  Thyme and hinny and heather,
Jeniper, birk and fern,
  Rose in the lown June weather.

It minded me o' auld days,
  When I wandered barefit there,
Guddlin' troot in the burns,
  Howkin' the tod frae his lair.

If a' the hills were graves
  There was peace for the folk aneath
And peace for the folk abune,
  And life in the hert o' death. . . .

   .   .   .   .   .   .

Up frae the howe o' the glen
  Cam the murmur o' wells that creep
To swell the heids o' the burns,
  And the kindly voices o' sheep.

And the cry o' a whaup on the wing,
  And a plover seekin' its bield. —
And oot o' my crazy lugs
  Went the din o' the battlefield.

   .   .   .   .   .   .

I flang me doun on my knees
  And I prayed as my hert wad break,
And I got my answer sune,
  For oot o' the nicht God spake.

As a man that wauks frae a stound
  And kens but a single thocht,
Oot o' the wind and the nicht
  I got the peace that I socht.

Loos and the Lammerlaw,
  The battle was feucht in baith,

Death was roond and abune,
    But life in the hert o' death.

A' the warld was a grave,
    But the grass on the graves was green,
And the stanes were bields for hames,
    And the laddies played atween.

Kneelin' aside the cairn
    On the heather and thymy sod,
The place I had kenned as a bairn,
    I made my peace wi' God.

The Great Ones   *(1916)*

Taken from *Poems Scots and English* (1917).

Ae morn aside the road frae Bray
    I wrocht my squad to mend the track;
A feck o' sodgers passed that way
    And garred me often straucht my back.

By cam a General on a horse,
    A jinglin' lad on either side.
I gie'd my best salute of course,
    Weel pleased to see sic honest pride.

And syne twae Frenchmen in a cawr —
    Yon are the lads to speel the braes;
They speldered me inch-deep wi' glaur
    And verra near ran ower my taes.

And last the pipes, and at their tail
    Oor gaucy lads in martial line.
I stopped my wark and cried them hail,
    And wished them weel for auld lang syne.

An auld chap plooin' on the muir
  Ne'er jee'd his heid nor held his han',
But drave his furrow straucht and fair, —
  Thinks I, "But ye're the biggest man."

Fisher Jamie   *(1916)*

This is one of Buchan's best-known poems and has been anthologised many times. It first appeared in *Poems Scots and English* (1917) and subsequently appeared in *Northern Numbers* (1920), *A St Andrews Treasury* (1920), *An Anglers Garland Of Fields, Rivers, and Other Country Contentments* (1920), and *A Book of 20th Century Verse* (1920), *The Northern Muse* (1924) and *The Scots Book* (1935). It is also included in *The Clearing House* (1946), and *Mr Buchan Writer* (1949) and two verses are quoted in *Benham's Book of Quotations* (1948).

Puir Jamie's killed. A better lad
  Ye wouldna find to busk a flee
Or burn a pule or weild a gad
  Frae Berwick to the Clints o' Dee.

And noo he's in a happier land. —
  It's Gospel truith and Gospel law
That Heaven's yett maun open stand
  To folk that for their country fa'.

But Jamie will be ill to mate;
  He lo'ed nae music, kenned nae tunes
Except the sang o' Tweed in spate,
  Or Talla loupin' ower its linns.

I sair misdoot that Jamie's heid
  A croun o' gowd will never please;
He liked a kep o' dacent tweed
  Whaur he could stick his casts o' flees.

If Heaven is a' that man can dream
  And a' that honest herts can wish,
It maun provide some muirland stream,
  For Jamie dreamed o' nocht but fish.

And weel I wot he'll up and speir
   In his bit blate and canty way,
Wi' kind Apostles standin' near
   Whae in their time were fishers tae.

He'll offer back his gowden croun
   And in its place a rod he'll seek,
And bashfu'-like his herp lay doun
   And speir a leister and a cleek.

For Jims had aye a poachin' whim;
   He'll sune grow tired, wi' lawfu' flee
Made frae the wings o' cherubim,
   O' castin' ower the Crystal Sea. . . .

I picter him at gloamin' tide
   Steekin' the backdoor o' his hame
And hastin' to the waterside
   To play again the auld auld game;

And syne wi' saumon on his back,
   Catch't clean against the Heavenly law,
And Heavenly byliffs on his track,
   Gaun linkin' doun some Heavenly shaw.

149

The 'Lusitania' Waits   *(1916)*

Taken from *Mystery Ships* by Alfred Noyes. There is some doubt regarding this story being one by John Buchan. However, Robert Blanchard in his Supplement to *The First Editions of John Buchan* (1987) notes: 'Buchan's story has not been positively identified, but, judging by style and content, is probably the one on pp.113–33, entitled "The Lusitania Waits" which also contains two poems.'

On a stormy winter's night three skippers are discussing the news, and Captain Morgan is asked to read a poem from the *Gazette*:

Long, long ago He said,
He who could wake the dead,
   And walk upon the sea —
   "Come follow Me.

"Leave your brown nets and bring
Only your hearts to sing,
   Only your souls to pray,
   Rise, come away.

"Shake out your spirit-sails,
And brave those wilder gales,
   And I will make you then
   Fishers of men."

Was this, then, what He meant?
Was this His high intent,
   After two thousand years
   Of blood and tears?

God help us, if we fight
For right and not for might.
   God help us if we seek
   To shield the weak.

Then, though His heaven be far
From this blind welter of war,
   He'll bless us on the sea
   From Calvary.

The three skippers then set off for trawler duty and another poem is recited.

WIRELESS

Now to those who search the deep,
  Gleam of Hope and Kindly Light,
Once, before you turn to sleep,
  Breathe a message through the night.
Never doubt that they'll receive it.
Send it, once, and you'll believe it.

Wrecks that burn against the stars,
  Decks where death is wallowing green,
Snare the breath among the spars,
  Hear the flickering threads between,
Quick, through all the storms that blind them,
Quick with worlds that rush to find them.

Think you these aerial wires
  Whisper more than spirits may?
Think you that our strong desires
  Touch no distance when we pray?
Think you that no wings are flying
  'Twixt the living and the dying?

Inland, here, upon your knees,
  You shall breathe from urgent lips,
Round the ships that guard your seas,
  Fleet on fleet of angel ships;
Yea, the guarded may so bless them
That no terrors can distress them.

You shall guide the darkling prow,
  Kneeling thus — and far inland —
You shall touch the storm-beat brow
  Gently as a spirit-hand.
Even a blindfold prayer may speed them,
And a little child may lead them.

151

Alastair Buchan *(1917)*

The following verses were written by John Buchan for a privately printed booklet to mark the death of his youngest brother at the Battle of Arras. It appeared in the 1936 edition of *Poems Scots and English* and a few verses were included in *Unforgettable, Unforgotten* (1945), the autobiography of John Buchan's sister Anna Buchan.

A.E.B.
Born 12th June, 1894
Died of Wounds received at Arras, 9th April, 1917

I

A mile or two from Arras town
 The yellow moorland stretches far,
And from its crest the roads go down
 Like arrows to the front of war.

All day the laden convoys pass,
 The sunburnt troops are swinging by,
And far above the trampled grass
 The droning planes climb up the sky.

In April when I passed that way
 An April joy was in the breeze;
The hollows of the woods were gay
 With slender-stalked anemones.

The horn of Spring was faintly blown,
 Bidding a ransomed world awake,
Nor could the throbbing batteries drown
 The nesting linnets in the brake.

And as I stood beside the grave,
 Where 'mid your kindly Scots you lie,
I could not think that one so brave,
 So glad of heart, so kind of eye.

Had found the deep and dreamless rest,
 Which men may crave who bear the scars
Of weary decades on their breast,
 And yearn for slumber after wars.

You scarce had shed your boyhood's years,
　　In every vein the blood ran young,
Your soul uncramped by ageing fears,
　　Your tales untold, your songs unsung.
　　.　　　.　　　.　　　.　　　.　　　.

As if my sorrow to beguile,
　　I heard the ballad's bold refrain:
"I'll lay me downe and bleed a-while,
　　And then I'll rise and fight again."

II

Long, long ago, when all the lands
　　Were deep in peace as summer sea,
God chose His squires, and trained their hands
　　For those stern lists of liberty.

You made no careful plans for life,
　　Happy with dreams and books and friends,
Incurious of our worldly strife,
　　As dedicate to nobler ends;

Like some young knight, who kept his sword
　　Virgin from common broils that he
Might flesh it on the Paynim horde
　　When Richard stormed through Galilee.

I mind how on the hills of home
　　You ever lagged and strayed aside,
A brooding boy whose thoughts would roam
　　O'er gallant fates that might betide.

But not the wildest dreams of youth,
　　Born of the sunset and the spring,
Could match the splendour of the truth
　　That waited on your journeying —

The ancient city deep in night,
　　The wind among its crumbling spires;
The assembly in the chill twilight
　　Murky with ghosts of wayward fires;

The last brave words; the outward march;
    The punctual shells, whose ceaseless beat
Made the dark sky an echoing arch
    Pounded without by demon feet;

While with the morn wild April blew
    Her snows across the tortured mead,
The spring-time gales that once you knew
    In glens beside the founts of Tweed;

And then the appointed hour; the dread
    Gun-flare that turned the sleet to flame,
When, the long vigil o'er, you led
    Your men to purge the world of shame.

I know that in your soul was then
    No fear to irk or hate to mar,
But a strong peace and joy as when
    The Sons of God go forth to war.

You did not fail till you had won
    The utmost trench and knew the pride
Of a high duty nobly done
    And a great longing satisfied.

You left the line with jest and smile
    And heart that would not bow to pain —
I'll lay me down and bleed a-while,
    And then I'll rise and fight again.

III

We cannot grieve that youth so strong
    Should miss the encroaching frosts of age,
The sordid fears, the unnerving throng
    Of cares that are man's heritage.

A boy in years, you travelled far
    And found perfection in short space;
By the stern sacrament of war
    You grew in gifts and power and grace,

Until, with soul attuned and tried,
    You reached full manhood, staunch and free,
And bore a spirit o'er the tide
    Most ripe for immortality.

We cannot tell what grave pure light
    Illumes for you our earthly show,
What heavenly love and infinite
    Wisdom is yours; but this we know: —

That just beyond our senses' veil
    You dwell unseen in youth and joy,
Joy which no languid years can pale
    Youth which is younger than the boy.

Your kindly voice enhearten still,
    Your happy laughter is not dead,
And when we roam our Border hill
    You walk beside with lighter tread.

All day where lies your valiant dust
    The troops go by to hold the line;
They never steel for ward or thrust
    But you are with them, brother mine.

Still, still you list the ancient tunes,
    The comrade fire is with you yet;
Still, still you lead your worn platoons
    Beyond the farthest parapet.

And when to chaos and black night
    At last the broken eagles flee,
Your heart will know the stern delight
    Of his who succours liberty.

.   .   .   .   .   .

I stood beside your new-made grave,
    And as I mused my sorrow fled,
Save for those mortal thoughts that crave
    For sight of those whom men call dead.

I knew you moved in ampler powers,
    A warrior in a purer strife,
Walking that world that shall be ours
    When death has called us dead to life.

The rough white cross above your breast,
    The earth ungraced by flower or stone,
Are bivouac marks of those that rest
    One instant ere they hasten on.

More fit such grave than funeral pile,
    Than requiem dirge and ballad strain:
I'll lay me downe and bleed a-while,
    And then I'll rise and fight again.

The Kirk Bell *(1917)*

Taken from *Poems Scots and English* (1917), it also appears in *Poems of the First World War* (1993).

When oor lads gaed ower the tap
    It was nine o' a Sabbath morn.
I felt as my hert wad stap,
    And wished I had ne'er been born;
    I wished I had ne'er been born
For I feared baith the foe and mysel',
    Till there fell on my ear forlorn
The jow o' an auld kirk bell.
For a moment the guns were deid,
    Sae I heard it faint and far;
And that bell was ringin' inside my heid
    As I stauchered into the war.

I heard nae ither soun',
    Though the air was a wild stramash,
And oor barrage beat the grun'

Like the crack o' a cairter's lash,
   Like the sting o' lang whup lash;
And ilk breath war a prayer or an aith,
   And whistle and drone and crash
Made the pitiless sang o' death.
But in a' that deavin' din
   Like the cry o' the lost in Hell,
I was hearkenin' to a peacefu' tune
   In the jow o' a far-off bell.

I had on my Sabbath claes,
   And was steppin' doucely the gait
To the kirk on the broomy braes;
   I was standin' aside the yett,
   Crackin' aside the yett;
And syne I was singin' lood
   'Mang the lasses snod and blate
Wi' their roses and southernwood.
I hae nae mind o' the tex'
   For the psalm was the thing for me,
And I gied a gey wheen Huns their paiks
   To the tune o' auld "Dundee."

They tell me I feucht like wud,
   And I've got a medal to shaw,
But in a' that habble o' smoke and bluid
   My mind was far awa';
   My mind was far awa'
In the peace o' a simmer glen,
   Daunderin' hame ower the heathery law,
Wi' twae-three ither men. . . .
But sudden the lift grew red
   Ere we wan to the pairtin' place;
And the next I kenned I was lyin' in bed
   And a Sister washin' my face.

My faither was stench U.P.;
   Nae guid in Rome could he fin';
But, this war weel ower, I'm gaun back to see

157

That kirk ahint the line —
That kirk ahint oor line,
And siller the priest I'll gie
    To pray for the sauls o' the deid langsyne
Whae bigged the steeple for me.
It's no that I'm chief wi' the Pape,
    But I owe the warld to yon bell;
And the beadle that swung the rape
    Will get half a croun for himsel'.

Home Thoughts From Abroad   *(1917)*

Taken from *Poems Scots and English* (1917) it has also appeared in *A Scots Book*
(1935), *A Book Of Twentieth Century Scots Verse* (1932), and *The Clearing House*
(1946).

Aifter the war, says the papers, they'll no be content at hame,
The lads that hae feucht wi' death twae 'ear i' the mud and the
    rain and the snaw;
For aifter a sodger's life the shop will be unco tame;
    They'll ettle at fortune and freedom in the new lands far awa'.

No me!
By God! No me!
Aince we hae lickit oor faes
And aince I get oot o' this hell
For the rest o' my leevin' days
I'll mak a pet o' mysel'.
I'll haste me back wi' an Eident fit
And settle again in the same auld bit.
And oh! the comfort to snowk again
The reek o' my mither's but-and-ben,
The wee box-bed and the ingle neuk
And the kail-pat hung frae the chimley-heuk!
I'll gang back to the shop like a laddie to play,
Tak doun the shutters at skreigh o' day,
And weigh oot floor wi' a carefu' pride,

And hear the clash o' the countraside.
I'll wear for ordinar' a roond hard hat,
A collar and dicky and black cravat.
If the weather's wat I'll no stir ootbye
Wi'oot an umbrella to keep me dry.
I think I'd better no tak a wife —
I've had a' the adventure I want in life. —
But at nicht, when the doors are steeked, I'll sit,
While the bleeze loups high frae the aiken ruit,
And smoke my pipe aside the crook.
And read in some douce auld-farrant book;
Or crack wi' Davie and mix a rummer,
While the auld wife's pow nid-nods in slum'er;
And hark to the winds gaun tearin' bye
And thank the Lord I'm sae warm and dry.

When simmer brings the lang bricht e'en,
I'll dauner doun to the bowling-green,
Or delve my yaird and my roses tend
For the big floo'er-show in the next back-end.
Whiles, when the sun blinks aifter rain,
I'll tak my rod and gang up the glen;
Me and Davie, we ken the pules
Whaur the troot grow great in the hows o' the hills;
And, wanderin' back when the gloamin' fa's
And the midges dance in the hazel shaws,
We'll stop at the yett ayont the hicht
And drink great wauchts o' the scented nicht,
While the hoose lamps kin'le raw by raw
And a yellow star hings ower the law.
Davie will lauch like a wean at a fair
And nip my airm to mak certain shure
That we're back frae yon place o' dule and dreid,
To oor ain kind warld —

But Davie's deid!
Nae mair gude nor ill can betide him.
We happit him doun by Beaumont toun,
And the half o' my hert's in the mools aside him.

Fragment of an ode in Praise
of the Royal Scots Fusiliers   *(1917)*

Buchan took a close interest in the Royal Scots Fusiliers. His brother, Alastair, was killed serving with them in 1917; one of his best-known fictional characters Geordie Hamilton is a member of the regiment, and in 1925 Buchan wrote their regimental history. The poem first appeared in *Poems Scots and English* (1917).

Ye'll a' hae heard tell o' the Fusilier Jocks,
 The famous auld Fusilier Jocks!
 They're as stieve as a stane,
 And as teuch as a bane
 And as gleg as a pack o' muircocks.
They're maistly as braid as they're lang,
And the Gairman's a pump off the fang
 When he faces the fire in their ee.
 They're no verra bonny,
 I question if ony
 Mair terrible sicht ye could see
Than a chairge o' the Fusilier Jocks.
 It gars Hindenburg swear
 "*Gott in Himmel*, nae mair
O' thae sudden and scan'alous shocks!"
 And the cannon o' Krupp
 Ane and a' they shut up
Like a pentit bit jaick-in-the-box,
At the rush o' the Fusilier Jocks.

The Kaiser he says to his son
 (The auld ane that looks like a fox) —
 "I went ower far
 When I stertit this war,
 Forgettin' the Fusilier Jocks.
I could manage the French and Italians and Poles,
The Russians and Tartars and yellow Mongols,
The Serbs and the Belgians, the English and Greeks,
And even the lads that gang wantin' the breeks;
But what o' thae Fusilier Jocks,
That stopna for duntin' and knocks?
 They'd rin wi' a yell

Ower the plainstanes o' Hell;
They're no men ava — they are rocks!
    They'd gang barefit
    Through the Bottomless Pit,
And they'll tak Berlin in their socks, —
Will the terrible Fusilier Jocks!" . . . .

The Return   *(1918)*

This previously unpublished poem was found in the archives of Kings College, Aberdeen University. It is referenced as by John Buchan, though there is a doubt regarding its authenticity. A small single sheet of paper reads:

> To the Officers, Non-Commissioned Officers and Men, who have fought in the Great War, which commenced on 4th August 1914 and ceased on 11th November 1918, the following lines are respectfully dedicated:

Haud up your heid, auld Scotland, ance again, an' tune your voice,
An' owre your heather hills an' dales wi' ilka ane rejoice,
For news hae jist been sent aroond, tae say that war will cease;
An' ance again, wi' a' the warld, we'll settle doon in peace.

Fowre years, ay, nearly five, since first oor laddies gaed awa',
Fine gallant youths, wha gaed in answer tae their country's ca',
An' oh, the wistfu' yearnings in oor he'rts for them doth burn,
As they across the seas frae bloody warfare noo return.

Wi' fond embrace an' wi' a kindly welcome let us greet
Thae worn an' bloodstained battered sons, wha mairch alang the street,
For nicht an' day, thro' muckle strife, they've feuchin' tae be free,
An' noo deserve a' due respeck frae sic as you an' me.

The ruthless han' o' war on maist o' them has left its trace,
An' as we gaze upon each wasted form an' haggard face,
The pallid cheeks, the sunken een, are sichts that mak' us grieve,
As weel as yon auld tattered tunic wi' the empty sleeve.

Hail to thee! Scotland's noblest sons, we'll revel ower your deeds,
An' noo confer the highest honours aye upon your heids,
For a' the eerie 'oors upon the battlefield ye've spent,
An' a' the bitter hardships which at hame we've never kent.

Beside the bleezin' ingle-nook o' ilka Scottish vale,
Wi' eagerness we'll gether roond an' listen tae your tale,
An', maybe, ye'll forgie us, if we chance tae drap a tear,
When ower-cam' wi' emotion at the bitter news we hear.

Jist tell us hoo, before the merc'less, brutal, bloody Huns,
Each comrade an' each brither stood sae bravely tae the guns?
Hoo Tam an' Jamie, Wull an' Geordie, chairged an' chairged again,
Until that fatal bullet left them dead upon the plain?

Then, let us bide a wee until oor thochts jist wan'er back,
Whaur cauld an' lifeless noo there lies on wild war's beaten track
Thae gallant laddies wha hae gien their wee bit span o' life,
In order tae preserve auld Scotland in the time o' strife.

See hoo yon aged mither, wha is burdened ower wi' care,
Sae eagerly expecks the son that will return nae mair;
The dark-e'ed lassie by yon stile an' secret trystin'-place
Whaur ne'er again she'll look upon that weel-remembered face.

No monumental tablet marks the spot where they are laid,
No murmer breaks the silence as they slumber in the shade,
For solitude reigns around each rudely fashioned bed,
While evening shadows spread their mantles o'er the fallen dead.

Close by the lonely mountain pass, where vultures love to soar,
Left on the dreary wilderness, where jackals nightly roar,
No beck'ning call can ever stir them from that peaceful sleep,
Since thro' the night God's angels silently their vigil keep.

But, weep not, gentle mothers, tho' they're parted from your side,
And o'er the barren wilds of Flanders scattered far and wide;
For now to all the World they are recorded with the brave
Who gain their reward behind the curtain of the grave.

To Vernon Watney   *(1923)*

Vernon Watney was a neighbour of the Buchans in Oxfordshire. His privately printed *Cornbury and the Forest of Wychwood* (1910) inspired Buchan's novel *Midwinter* (1923) which in turn Buchan dedicated to Watney.

> We two confess twin loyalties —
> Wychwood beneath the April skies
> Is yours, and many a scented road
> That winds in June by Evenlode.
> Not less when autumn fires the brake,
> Yours the deep heath by Fannich's lake,
> The corries where the dun deer roar
> And eagles wheel above Sgurr Mór.
> So I, who love with equal mind
> The southern sun, the northern wind,
> The lilied lowland water-mead
> And the grey hills that cradle Tweed,
> Bring you this tale which haply tries
> To intertwine our loyalties.

Sandy to Alasdair   *(1927)*

Taken from *Voices From The Hills*, a memento from the Gaelic Rally, published in 1927. It is introduced by a definition which reads:

> *Hieland* – a term of reproach, used in the Lowlands to signify something freakish, wild, uncertain, barbarous.
>
> *Scots Dictionary*

> My faither cam frae Sanquhar ways,
>   My mither's folk frae Loudon hill,
> I played as a wean on the Cairnsmuir braes,
>   And got my lear at the Deuchrae schule.
> Weel I mind, when at ilk ran-dan
>   I'd tak the muir like a young peesweep,
> My faither sighed, and said he, "My man,
>   Ye're far ower Hieland to wark wi' sheep."

163

But the herding wasna the fate for me:
  Wi' the Fusil Jocks I went to war;
Sune we were flitted ayont the sea,
  Jinkin' death in the stour and the glaur.
There was lads frae the West and lads frae the North,
  Frae mill and muirland and pleugh and pit,
And the youngest callant frae 'yont the Forth
  Was far ower Hieland to yield a fit.

Yon day when, smoored wi' the deil's ain reeks,
  We broke ower Loos like a wave o' the sea,
Anither Sandy wi'oot the breeks
  Keepit me company knee to knee;
Roarin' words that nae man could ken,
  Through trench and wire we gae'd side by side,
And when I drapped like a shot greyhen
  He was far ower Hieland to let me bide.

Here's to ye, freend, whaure'er ye be!
  Atween us two we hae couped the dyke;
Gaelic for you and Lallan for me,
  But the back o' our heids is unco like.
Scotland's braid, and the differ's big,
  Lorn and Carrick are no the same;
But sune as the pipes play up their sprig
  We're a' ower Hieland to hunker at hame.

Ferris Greenslet *(1929)*

Buchan had met Ferris Greenslet, an editor with Houghton Mifflin, during the First World War and Greenslet became Buchan's regular American publisher for all his post war books. The two men shared a love of fishing and it is this theme that Buchan chose in his dedicatory verse to Greenslet in his novel *The Courts of the Morning* (1929). The poem was later included in the 1936 edition of *Poems Scots and English* and three verses are quoted in *John Buchan by his Wife and Friends* (1945).

The trout that haunts the Beaverkill
　Will flick the same sarcastic tail,
When badly struck, as him my skill
　Would vainly lure from Tweed or Kale.

The same old tremor of the spring
　Assails the heart of you and me;
Nor does the reel less blithely ring
　By Willowemoc than by Dee.

As bright the Ammonoosuc streams
　Dance through their silent scented woods
As those that fill my waking dreams
　In Hebridean solitudes.

Your land, old friend, is one with mine,
　Whate're may hap from time or tide,
While, with St Izaak the Divine,
　We worship at the waterside.

Oxford Prologizes   *(1930)*

Buchan was active with various heritage organisations, notably the Oxford Preservation Trust. He wrote this poem, printed in the *Times*, for a matinee hosted by the Trust at the Haymarket Theatre, 25 February 1930. The poem was later included in the 1936 edition of *Poems Scots and English*.

Welcome I give you, gentles all,
Who honour this, my carnival;
For mine the prose and mine the rhymes,
Mine the choragus and the mimes,
And not a word that's said or sung
But springs from Oxford pen or tongue.

From that first day when men descried
The double path o'er Isis' tide
And set a city by the fords,
Through the dark wars of books and swords,
I fenced a little citadel
Where might the gentler Muses dwell.
And not alone Athene reigned
Among my towers; Artemis deigned
To lead her dance; my youthful quire
Has heard Apollo tune his lyre;
Through tributary hamlets ran
The piping of the rustic Pan;
By Fyfield elm and Bampton plain
The morris-dancers wove their chain,
And masques with lute and virginal
Have greeted kings in Christ Church hall.
Though changed the times, the comic boot
Yet treads my boards; Euterpe's flute
Sounds still for chosen lass and lad;
And, when the bonfire lights the quad,
With flying hair the orgiast raves,
The cymbals clash, the thyrsus waves.

This day a graver purpose runs
Through these the revels of my sons.

'Tis not to grace some holy day,
Or band my young in summer play,
Or loose from Cardinal's purse the string,
Or win a smile from wandering King,
But ye my children, far and wide,
To call confederate to my side,
For the old love, for the old pride.

Where once the modest pilgrim strode,
Immodest myriads throng my road,
Not borne on horse or foot, but such
As nurse the inviolable clutch,
Devour the steep and scour the lea
With onward impulse all too free.
The rawest rufous cabins rise
Above my shy fritillaries;
My secret hills are cloven and scarred,
And narrower grows my zone of sward.
Wherefore, despoiled, I make my prayer
For succour to my children ere
Some dunce, not Scotus, fling his net
Of drab o'er my green coronet.

For centuries seven my questing sons
I drew by every road that runs.
Rough were the paths they paced of old,
The miry track by heath and wold.
By forest wilds and swollen streams,
In winter snows and April gleams.
They begged their bread and paid their score
With trifles from the Muses' store,
In many a wayside hostelry
With Peter Turph and Stephen Sly.
But, whether on weary feet they came,
By laggard coach, by rail or car,
From fields of home, from lands afar,
My guerdon was for each the same.
I gave them youth's divine surmise
Mirrored in my eternal eyes;
I gave them for a sanctuary

My cloisters, where enchantments lie
Unbroken since the Golden Age;
And, for an ampler heritage,
Green neighbour fields and quiet rills
Cradled by soft, deep-bosomed hills.
I gave them spell of antique arts,
And ancient dreams of seeking hearts.
And, as a panoply for strife,
Whate'er the sages taught of life.
But most I gave them loyalties,
The soul to dare, the wing to rise,
The dear companionships of youth,
And the clear eye that welcomes truth.

They came from far; farther they fared.
Whate'er man's venturous heart has dared,
So dared my sons; in toil and dearth
They blazed the untrodden trails of earth,
Harnessed the flood and tilled the sands,
Set gardens in the desert lands.
They freed the slave, and raised the mean.
And curbed the lawless, and made clean
The heart of darkness.
                                    On the grave
Of such no English grasses wave;
Ganges and Nile, not Isis keep
A vigil o'er their timeless sleep.
But in their toils they kept apart,
Deep in the treasury of the heart,
The thought of me, a charm to bless,
A palm-tree in the wilderness.
They saw beyond the sand dunes gleam
The summer deeps of Hinksey stream.
And breathed, when swamps lay dank and still,
An April wind on Cumnor hill.

Esto perpetua! This my plea
To all whose hearts are vowed to me.

My sons out of the world I draw,
And mould them to my gentle law,
And send them back to play their part
In court and senate, field and mart,
For ever mine, if once they hear
My secret whispered in their ear.
But for such task I needs must dwell
Out of the strife, a citadel
With warders at the outer gate,
A place enclosed, inviolate.
So may I in its purity
Preserve the truth that maketh free
From taint of narrow loss and gain; ·
So may my children still be fain
To hallow with their dreams my town,
The Tripled as the Violet Crown;
And, like the wise of old, to see
Some bloom of immortality
In the dear ways their youth has trod —
City of Cecrops — City of God.

The Magic Walking Stick   *(1932)*

This poem is given as an introduction to Buchan's children's story *The Magic Walking Stick* (1932). It is also printed in *The Clearing House* (1946).

"Magic," gasped the dull mind,
    When the harnessed earth and skies
Drew the nomads of their kind
    To uncharted emperies —
Whispers round the globe were sped,
    Construed was the planets' song.

But the little boy playing in the orchard said,
Conning his tale in the orchard said,
    "I knew it all along."

Power deduced from powerless dust,
    Nurture from the infertile grave;
Much the years may hold in trust,
    Space a thrall and Time a slave.
Hark the boasting of the wise:
    "First are we of those that know!"

But the little boy playing by the roadside cries,
Trundling his hoop by the roadside cries,
    "I said it long ago."

The Old Love   *(1941)*

At his death in February 1940 Buchan had just completed a children's book on Canadian history. The book was serialised in *Good Housekeeping* between February and July 1941 and published in America in August as *Lake of Gold* and in Britain three months later as *The Long Traverse*. Buchan included several of his own poems in the book, including 'The Spirit of the North' which had originally been the introduction to his Newdigate Prize Poem on the *Pilgrim Fathers* written over forty years earlier.

The little countries are shaped by men
    And moulded by human hands. —
But you cannot trace on my ancient face
    The scars of the little lands.
They come, they pass, like shadows on grass,
    Or a child's play on the sands.

Dawns and dusks and storms and suns
    Have spun my tapestry,
From the lakes of the South to the snows of the North,
    From the East to the Western sea,
Which lays its arts on my children's hearts,
    And brings them back to me.

Far they may travel and fine they may fare,
    And new loves come with the years;
But a scent or a sound will call them back,

And my voice will speak in their ears,
And the old love, the deep love,
   Will dim their eyes with tears.

To each will come a remembered scene,
   Bright as in childhood's day;
Dearer than all that lies between
   Those blue hills far away.

They will remember the fragile Springs
   Ere the horn of Summer blows,
And the rapturous Falls when the year burns out
   In ashes of gold and rose,
And the Winters brimmed with essential light
   From the crystal heart of the snows. —

The tides run in from the opal seas
   Through the thousand isles of the West,
And the winds that ride the mountain side
   Ruffle the tall trees' crest —
Forests old when the world was young,
   And dark as a raven's breast.

Morning leaps o'er the Prairie deeps,
   Girdled with gold and fire;
In the hot noon the cornland sleeps,
   And the drowsy crickets choir; —
The dews fall, and the sun goes down
   To a fierce mid-ocean pyre.

In the wild hay mead the dun deer feed
   And the long hill-shadows lie;
The regiments of prick-eared firs
   March to the saffron sky;
There is no sound but the lap of the lake,
   And at even the loon's cry.

The cold Atlantic gnaws by my feet
   As a famished wolf at a bone,
The wind-blown terns old tales repeat
   Of sailormen dead and gone,

And the apple-blossom and salt spray meet
  On the skirts of Blomidon.

Mile-wide rivers roll to the sea,
  And my lakes have an ocean's moods,
But the little streams are the streams for me
  That dance through the scented woods,
And by bar and shingle and crag and lea
  Make song in the solitudes.

Far and wide my children roam,
  And new loves come with the years,
But a scent or a sound will bring them home,
  And my voice will speak in their ears,
And the old love, the deep love,
  Will dim their eyes with tears.

ॐ   ॐ   ॐ

The Forerunners *(1941)*

You may follow far in the blue-goose track
  To the lands where spring is in mid-July;
You may cross to the unmapped mountains' back,
  To lakes unscanned by the trapper's eye.
You may trace to its lair the soft Chinook,
  And the North Wind trail to the Barren's floor;
But you'll always find, or I'm much mistook,
  That some old Frenchman's done it before.

You may spirit wealth from despisèd dust,
  Gold from the refuse and gems from the spoil;
You may draw new power from the torrent's thrust,
  And bend to your use the ocean's toil;
You may pierce to Nature's innermost nook,
  And pluck the heart of her secret lore;
But you'll always find, or I'm much mistook
  That some old Frenchman's done it before.

You may hunt all day for the fitting word,
    The aptest phrase and the rightful tune,
Beating the wood for the magic bird,
    Dredging the pond to find the moon.
And when you escape (in the perfect book)
    From the little less and the little more,
You're sure to find, or I'm much mistook,
    That some old Frenchman's done it before.

Cadieux   *(1941)*

"Petit rocher de la haute montagne
Je viens ici finir cette campagne."

Little rock of the mountainside,
Here I rest from all my pride.
Sweet echo, hear my cry;
I lay me down to die.

Say to my dear ones, nightingale,
My love for them can never fail.
My faith has known no stain,
But they see me not again.

Now the world has dimmed its face,
Saviour of men I seek Thy grace.
Sweet Virgin ever blest,
Gather me to thy breast.

Chansons   *(1941)*

What are the songs that Cadieux sings
Out in the woods when the axe-blade rings?
Whence the word and whence the tune
Which under the stars the boatmen croon?

173

Some are the games that children play
When they dance in rings on a noon in May,
And the maiden choir sings high and low
Under the blossomy orchard snow.
Some are the plaints of girls forlorn,
For lovers lost and pledges torn,
Told at eve to the evening star,
When the lit *tourelle* is a lamp afar.
Some are sung 'neath the dreaming trees
In modish garden pleasances,
Where a silken Colin indites his ode
To a shepherdess hooped and furbelowed,
And fat carp swim in the fountain's deep,
And the cares of the world have gone to sleep.
And some are the lays of the good green earth,
Of sunburnt toil and hobnailed mirth,
Where Time is loth to turn the page,
And lingers as in the Golden Age.

That is the tongue that Cadieux speaks
In his *bottes sauvages* and his leathern breeks —
Old sweet songs of the far-off lands,
Norman orchards and Breton sands,
Chicken-skin fans and high-heeled shoon, —
Squires and ladies under the moon, —
Which the night wind carries swift and keen
To the ears of the wolf and the wolverine,
And every beast in the forest's law, —
And maybe a prowling Iroquois.

The Blessed Isles   *(1941)*

The air is quiet as the grave,
   With never a wandering breeze
Or the fall of a breaking wave
   In the hollow shell of the seas.
Ocean and heavens are a maze
   Of hues like a peacock's breast,
And far in the rainbow haze
   Lie the Isles of the West.

Uist and Barra and Lews —
   Honey-sweet are the words —
They set my heart in a muse
   And give me wings like a bird's.
Darlings, soon will I fly
   To the home of the tern and the bee,
And deep in the heather lie
   Of the Isles of the Sea.

But they say there are other lands
   For him who has heart and will,
Whiter than Barra's sands,
   Greener than Icolmkill,
Where the cool sweet waters flow,
   And the White Bird sings in the skies
Such songs as immortals know
   In the fields of Paradise.

So I'll launch my boat on the seas
   And sail o'er the shadowy deep,
Past the Island of Apple Trees
   And the little Island of Sheep,
And follow St Brandan's way
   Far into the golden West,
Till I harbour at the close of day
   In the Isles of the Blest.

Horse or Gun? *(1941)*

Which shall I choose of two excellent things,
Big Dog — or the Stick-that-sings?

On Big Dog's back I can eat up the ground,
Faster than an antelope, stealthy as hound.
Two-Suns think that I hunt remote,
When my knife is a yard from Two-Suns' throat.
The buffalo dream that the plain is clear —
In an hour my bow will twang in their ear.
Who owns Big Dog is a mighty brave,
For the earth is his squaw, and the wind his slave.

With the Stick-that-sings all soft and still
I pick my lair and I make my kill.
Shield nor sentry can cramp the wings
Of the death that flies from the Stick-that-sings.
Man and beast I smite from afar,
And they know not their foe in that secret war.
Big dog is a marvel beyond dispraise,
But *he* dies at the breath of the Stick-that-slays.

Wherefore, though both are marvellous things,
My voice shall be for the Stick-that-sings.

Things to Remember *(1941)*

Child, if you would live at ease
Learn these few philosophies.

If you fear a bully's frown,
Smite him briskly on the crown.
If you're frightened of the dark,
Go to bed without a spark
To light up the nursery stairs,

And be sure to say your prayers.
If your pony's raw and new,
Show that you can stick like glue.
If the fence seems castle-high,
Throw your heart across and try.
Whatsoever risk portends,
Face it and you'll soon be friends.

But though many perils you dare
Mingle fortitude with care.
Do not tempt the torrent's brim
Till you've really learned to swim.
Do not climb the mountain snow
If inclined to vertigo.
Do not let yourself be seen
Mother bear and cubs between;
Or essay your marksman's skill
On a grizzly couched uphill, —
Else this mortal stage you'll leave
And your parents fond will grieve.

The Foot-Traveller   *(1941)*

At first we went on our own flat feet,
   Moccasined, booted, or bare as at birth,
Brisk in frost and laggard in heat,
   Bound for the uttermost ends of the earth.
Hill and prairie and deep muskegs
   Were covered in turn by our aching legs.

We have sailed on the Ultimate Seas,
   We have tramped o'er the Infinite Plain;
We have carried our pack to the icebergs and back,
   And by ——* we will go there again!

We broke the trail on the winter crust,
   Husky and malamute trotting behind;

Our pack-train coughed in the alkali dust,
    And strained in the passes against the wind.
In the prairie loam, on the world's high roof,
From dawn to dusk we padded the hoof.

Canoe and bateau speeded our way,
    But half the time we were wading the creek,
And the longest portage fell on the day
    When our bellies were void and our legs were weak.
Like docile mules we shouldered the pack
And carried a wonderful weight on our back.
        .   .   .   .   .   .

Now behold has a miracle brought
    Ease to our legs and speed to the way;
Outboards chug where canoemen wrought,
    A month's toil now is a morning's play;
The mountain track is a metalled road
And motors carry the pack-train's load.

Through the conquered air we speed to our goal;
    Swamps and forests are dim beneath;
The virgin peak and the untrod Pole
    Fade behind like a frosty breath.
Freed from the toil of our ancient wars,
We outpace the winds and outface the stars.

Yet — when we come to the end of our quest,
    The last grim haul in the gully's heart,
The uttermost ice of the mountain's crest,
    The furthest ridge where the waters part,
The lode deep hid in the cypress fen
A thousand miles from the eyes of men —

Then we return to our fathers' ways,
    For help there is none from earth or heaven;
Once again as in elder days
    We are left with the bodies that God has given.
At the end the first and the last things meet
And we needs must go on our own flat feet.

We have sailed on the Ultimate Seas,
  We have tramped o'er the Infinite Plain;
We have carried our pack to the icebergs and back,
  And by —— * we will go there again!

* Expletive according to taste

Qu'appelle?   *(1941)*

Taken from *The Long Traverse*, (in the USA — *The Lake Of Gold*), both published in 1941. The poem also appears in *The Clearing House* (1946), and was printed in *Good Housekeeping* magazine in July 1941.

>   *Qu'appelle?*
> A whisper steals through the sunburnt grasses;
> Faint as a twilight wind it passes,
>   Broken and slow,
>   Soft and low,
> And the heart responds like a beaten bell;
> For the voice comes out of the ancient deeps
> Where the blind, primordial Terror sleeps,
> And hark! It is followed by soft footfalls!
>   *Who calls?*
>
>   *Qu'appelle?*
> What is it stirs the cedars high,
> When there is no wind in all the sky,
>   And plays queer tunes
>   On the saskatoons,
> Subtler airs than the ear can tell?
> The evening breeze? But wise men warn
> That the tune and the wind are elfin-born,
> And lure the soul to uncanny things.
>   *Who sings?*
>
>   *Qu'appelle?*
> The world is empty of stir and sound,
> Not a white fox barks in the void profound;

On the Elder Ice
Old Silence lies,
Older than Time and deep as Hell.
Yet a whisper creeps as a mist from a fen
Which is not the speech of articulate men,
And the hunter flees like a startled bird.
Whose word?

Fragments

The following section contains fragments of poetry which have been extracted from books, stories and essays written by John Buchan. Every care has been taken to verify their authenticity. Buchan, however, used many poetical quotations throughout his works and, as the astute reader will perceive, some of these fragments are not his own.

'Gentlemen of Leisure' *(1894)*

Taken from Buchan's essay collection *Scholar-Gipsies* (1896). The story, Buchan's second published work, appeared in *MacMillan's Magazine* in January 1894. Buchan makes a comparison between a country parson and a tramp. In his younger day the parson had been a great sportsman:

> But most his measured words of praise
> Caressed the angler's easy ways —
> His idly meditative days,
> > His rustic diet.

The tramp enjoyed the same sporting pleasures, but most of all the forced marches, which hardships tested him beyond the limits of his strength.
    His days, certainly, were not all spent in a:

> > ditch supine,
> Or footing it over the sunlit lea.

'On Cademuir Hill' *(1894)*

This short story was first published in December 1894 in the *Glasgow University Magazine* while Buchan was in his final year at the University. The Gamekeeper of Cademuir, 'on his way to discuss foxes with a shepherd', finds a poachers trap and, unfortunately, pins himself in it. He cannot free himself and, falling into a panic, he thinks of this drinking song:

> When the hoose is innin' round about,
> > It's time eneuch to flit;
> For we've lippened aye to Providence,
> > And sae will we yet.

'Musa Piscatrix' *(1896)*

Buchan dedicated this book of fishing poems to a fellow Borderer and writer Andrew Lang, with the following verse:

> Who glories to have thrown in air
> High over arm, the trembling reed,
> By Ale and Kail, by Till and Tweed.

'May-fly fishing' (Scholar Gipsies) *(1896)*

An expedition where,

> It is useless to try for him, so we pass by on the other side, quoting to ourselves the song of the contented man:

> > For if he be not for me,
> > What care I for whom he be?

'Afternoon' (Scholar Gipsies) *(1896)*

This essay concerns the travels of a Jacobite cavalier, during which he meets a Lady. She tells the young wanderer of town life and how people believe

> . . . stories about Hector, Ulysses, William Tell and Arthur are nonsense. She repeated softly to herself:

> > *Praetulerim scriptor delirus inersque videri,*
> > *Dum mea delectent mala me vel denique fallant,*
> > *Quam sapere et ringi.*

'An Individualist' (Scholar Gipsies)   *(1896)*

A wanderer in the hills meets up with a tramp who asks him for the time of day. The 'tramp' says

> . . . some men are born to be good citizens. Others lack the domestic virtues. How does the thing go?:
>
> > *Non illum tectis ullae, non moenibus urbes*
> > *Accepere, neque ipse manus feritate dedisset,*
> > *Pastorum et solis exegit montibus aevum.*

'Nuces Relictae' (Scholar Gipsies)   *(1896)*

This essay is introduced by the following Latin lines:

> *Jam tristis nucibus puer relictis*
> *Clamoso revocatur a magistro.*

'At the Article of Death'   *(1897)*

Buchan's third story in *The Yellow Book*, 'At the Article of Death' was first published there in January 1897 and later in the collection *Grey Weather (1899)*. This tale is introduced by the following Latin lines:

> *Nullum*
> *Sacra caput Proserpina fugit.*

At the onset of death a shepherd recalls a charm against evil fairies,

> which the little folk of the moors still speak at their play,
>
> > "Wearie, Ovie, gang awa',
> > Dinna show your face at a',
> > Ower the muir and down the burn,
> > Wearie, Ovie, ne'er return."

'John Burnet of Barns' (1898)

John Burnet, the central character of Buchan's historical novel *John Burnet of Barns*, would often rouse the 'wildest anger' in his tutor Master Robert Porter by

'. . . singing a profane song of my own making:

"O, ken ye his Reverence Minister Tam
Wi' a heid like a stot and a face like a ram?"

Nicol Plenderlieth and John Burnet are aboard a vessel bound for the low countries, when the Captain begins to hum a ditty:

Tam o' the Linn and a' his bairns
Fell into the fire and ilk ither's airms.
"Eh," quoth the hinmost, "I have a het skin,"
"It's better below," quo' Tam o' the Linn.

Later Nicol

began to sing with a great affectation of grief:

The craw killed the pussie O,
The craw killed the pussie O,
The wee bit kittlin' sat and grat
In Jennie's wee bit hoosie O.

'A Lost Lady of Old Years' (1898–99)

This fragment is taken from the novel of this title, published in 1899. It was originally serialised in *Today*, in fifteen parts, between November 1898 and February 1899. Francis Birkehshaw meets a pedlar while travelling through Nairnshire. The pedlar speaks Scots easily and after answering his question with 'Sodgers, ay; sodgers mony' goes on with his singing:

"If ye hae plenty and winna gie,
Besouthen, Besouthen!
The deil will get ye when ye dee,
And awa by southron toun!"

After telling Francis, 'the Prince, as ye ca' him, he's in Inverness, but Cumberland's at Nairn —', the pedlar goes down the road singing:

> "My shoon are made o' the red-coo's hide,
>   Besouthen, Besouthen!
> My feet are cauld, I canna bide,
>   And awa by southron toun!"

'The Herd of Standlan' *(1899)*

First published in the magazine *Black and White* this story was later included in *Grey Weather* (1899). It is introduced by:

> "When the wind is nigh and the moon is high
>   And the mist on the riverside,
> Let such as fare have a very good care
>   Of the Folk who come to ride.
> For they may meet with the riders fleet
>   Who fare from the place of dread;
> And hard it is for a mortal man
>   To sort at ease with the Dead."

The Ballad Of Grey Weather

'Streams of Water in the South' *(1899)*

Buchan included this story in both *Grey Weather* (1899) and his short story collection *The Moon Endureth* (1912). The story is introduced with these lines, taken from Psalm 76:

> "Like streams of water in the South
>   Our bondage, Lord, recall."

'The Far Islands' *(1899)*

'The Far Islands' was published in *Blackwood's Magazine* in November 1899 and included in the Buchan short story collection *The Watcher by the Threshold* (1902). It is introduced by two lines:

> "Lady Alice, Lady Louise,
> Between the wash of the tumbling seas — "

'Prince Charles Edward' *(1900)*

Published first in *Blackwood's Magazine* in October 1900, the essay was included in Buchan's collection *Some Eighteenth Century Byways* (1908). In it Buchan suggests that

> all who ever loved him . . . regretted that he had not been dear to the gods,
>
> > "To have fallen where Keppoch fell,
> > With the war-pipe loud in his ear."

'The African Colony' *(1903)*

In this volume John Buchan discourses on the history of Africa, its colonisation, its natural qualities, and notes:

> . . . there comes a new feeling of the scene, as of something old, not new, decaying rather than undeveloped, which, joined with the moist heat, makes the place
>
> > "A land
> > In which it seemed always afternoon,
> > All round the coast the languid air did swoon,
> > Breathing like one that hath a weary dream."

and further:

> . . . but it is the history of cosmic forces, of the cycle of the seasons, of storms and suns and floods, the joys and sorrows of the natural world.

> "Lo, for there among the flowers and grasses
> Only the mightier movement sounds and passes;
> Only winds and rivers,
> Life and death."

and later:

> For here, as in all places of subtle and profound beauty, there is need of the seeing eye and the understanding heart.

> "We receive but what we give,
> And in our life alone does Nature live;
> Ours is her wedding garment, ours her shroud!
> And would we aught behold of higher worth
> Than that inanimate cold world allowed
> To the poor loveless, ever-anxious crowd,
> Ah! from the soul itself must issue forth
> A light, a glory, a fair luminous cloud
> Enveloping the earth."

'A Lodge in the Wilderness' *(1906)*

The guests in Buchan's country house discussion novel of this title discuss Imperialism and Lord Launceston quotes:

> Not till the hours of light return,
> All we have built do we discern.

After the dinner one of the ladies sings to a

> melody of her own making, very wild and tender;

Car c'est chose supreme
D'aimer sans qu'on vous aime,
D'aimer toujours, quand même,
Sans cesse,
D'une amour incertaine,
Plus noble d'etre vaine,
Et j'aime la lointaine
Princesse!

Lady Flora Brune and Hugh, at the end of their three week trek, are discussing the journey and their idea of 'Nirvana' when Flora remembers Sir Edward's poem, 'something about the "wind in his teeth"?' Hugh then quotes a verse from 'The Strong Man Armed' (see page 36).

Hugh, during the final discussions, is attempting to supply a philosophical creed to Flora in respect of Imperialism, and quotes from 'Antiphilus of Byzantium' (see page 37).

Lord Appin, in putting to the party the fundamental question in Imperialism, suggests

. . . the humblest among us . . . aspire for a moment to:

'the shining table-lands
To which our God Himself is moon and sun.'

Lord Appin, in summarising the conclusions of the many philisophical discussions, appeals to the

aristocracy of ambition, those who can think clearly, feel cleanly, and act whole-heartedly

'patrician spirits that refine
Their flesh to fire and issue like a flame
On brave endeavours.'

'The New Doctrine of Empire' (1907)

'The New Doctrine of Empire' first appeared in the *Scottish Review* in May 1907. A collection of the pieces, including this one, were published as *Comments and Characters* in October 1940. In the article Buchan refers to the Imperial Conference and

ties of kinship and tradition, but it is well also to remember that

> "The glories of our blood and State
> Are shadows, not substantial things,"

'The Alps' (1907)

This article first appeared in the *Scottish Review* in July 1907 and was included in *Comments and Characters* (1940). Buchan considers the advantages of camping out-of-doors:

Have one friend to help you, and

> "Enlargéd winds that cool the flood
> Know no such liberty."

You can pitch or strike camp where you please.

'Lady Louisa Stuart' (1908)

Taken from *Some Eighteenth Century Byways* (1908), the essay appeared first in the *Quarterly Review* during July the same year. Buchan discusses the writings of Lady Louisa Stuart on the subject of Sir Walter Scott, and how they give

'a more noble picture of the man, who was assuredly no

> pipe for Fortune's finger
> To sound what stop she please

'The Apocalyptic Style' *(1908)*

This essay appeared first in *Blackwood's Magazine* in October 1908 and was republished in *Some Eighteenth Century Byways* (1908). Discussing twentieth century life, literature, and thought, Buchan refers to Burke,

> at the height of his great argument, his metaphors and appeals which;

> "tease us out of thought,
> As doth eternity."

'Space' *(1911)*

One of Buchan's best-known characters, Sir Edward Leithen, made his debut in the short story 'Space' published in *Blackwood's Magazine* in May 1911 and *Living Age* the following month. It was later included in *The Moon Endureth* (1912). Leithen tells the story of Hollond,

> a mathematical professor, who has exceptional ideas on "involution of space". He, Hollond, quotes the following verse:

> Within the region of the air,
> Compassed about with Heavens fair,
> Great tracts of lands there may be found,
>   Where many numerous hosts,
>   In those far distant coasts,
> For other great and glorious ends
> Inhabit, my yet unknown friends.

'Sir Walter Raleigh' *(1911)*

In this book, published during October 1911, Buchan says of Sir Walter Raleigh,

> like a great modern poet, he

> > Held we fall to rise, are baffled to fight better,
> > Sleep to wake.

'The Green Glen' *(1912)*

'The Green Glen' first appeared in *Blackwood's Magazine* in January 1912 and was one of the stories in *The Moon Endureth (1912)*. Buchan chose to include it in *Modern Short Stories* which he edited in 1926. The storyteller is on a fishing trip on the Lowland river Fawn. The Rhymer had

> honoured the Fawn with a couplet of doubtful Latin

> > *Ubi Faunis fluit*
> > *Spes mortalis ruit.*

And a translation of this verse:

> > Where Fawn flows
> > Man's hope goes.

'Salute to Adventurers' *(1915)*

Salute to Adventurers has several examples of Buchan's poetry, but when one of the central characters, Andrew Garvald, meets up with a stranger, 'who was either drunk or in good spirits', he is singing:

> > "We're a' dry wi' the drinkin' o't,
> > We're a' dry wi' the drinkin' o't.

The minister kissed the fiddler's wife,
And he couldna preach for thinkin' o't."

(Robert Burns)

Buchan also included in this volume an extract from his own poem 'The
Lady Cassilis' (see p. 57).

'The Achievement of France' *(1915)*

In the book *The Achievement of France* John Buchan discusses the rela-
tionship between the French and English forces and writes:

A sonnet by M. Maurice Allou, which I roughly translate, is proof of
the new unity of Western Europe.

OUR ALLIES THE ENGLISH

"We know not France," so ran their frank decreeing;
And we, we joyed not in their humours rude,
They praised our fire, but scorned our fortitude.
"Fog-bound their land," we said, "and dim their seeing."
But side by side deployed in truceless wars
Sudden our hearts are clear beyond surmising,
They know a France to the great days uprising:
We see beyond their fogs the ancient stars.

'Tis Kipling's spirit, fierce, unshackled, and bright,
His songs of deepest peace and ardent flame,
That in the eyes of her free warriors gleam.
And England, now thou look'st with heroes' sight,
Thou know'st, O fiery race whom none may tame,
That France has borne the sons of Corneille's dream.

193

'Nelson's History of the War'   *(1915–1919)*

There are several short verses in the twenty-four volumes of Nelson's History of the War.

Vol.I Chapter IV   January 1915

When recounting the muster of forces throughout the British Empire, it is said;

We had created a spiritual bond,

Which, softness' self, is yet the stuff
To hold fast where a steel chain snaps.

Vol.II Chapter XIII   March 1915

Tannenberg was the only battle in the first months of the war that in itself could be considered a complete and decisive victory by the Germans. Von Hindenburg had:

wrought
Upon the plan which pleased his boyish thought,

Vol.VI Chapter XLIII   July 1915

At Przasnysz the Russian soldiers were armed with only rifles and bombs, but under close quarter fighting they forced the enemy to retreat:

Back towards the northland and the night
The stricken eagles scattered from the field.

Vol.X Chapter LXXIII   February 1916

There come moments in a campaign when the high tide of an advance appears to be reached and the ebb begins. At the time it is imperceptible to the combatants of both sides. To the defence it seems that;

The enemy faints not nor faileth,
And as things have been they remain.

Vol.XIII Chapter XCVI   July 1916

In making a comparison between the current war in the European theatre with the conquest of the Cameroons, Buchan says the former is something new in history, new indeed in the whole history of war.

> Far other is this battle in the west
> Whereto we move, there when we strove in youth
> And brake the petty kings.

Vol.XIV Chapter CII   October 1916

Buchan writes of the death of Lord Kitchener, discusses his character, and introduces a 'free translation' of a poem which appeared in a journal published in the French trenches:

> Cypress nor yew shall weave for him their shade;
>   Cypress nor yew shall shield his quiet sleep;
> Marble must crack, and graven names must fade —
>   He for his tomb hath won the changeless deep.
> We mortal pilgrims bring our transient gift,
>   Fast-fading flowers, as garlands for his fame;
> But 'tis the tempest and the thunderous drift
>   That to eternity shall sound his name.

Vol.XVII Chapter CXXV   August 1917

During the closing months of 1916 people were seen

advancing from Picardy into the shadows of catastrophe —

> The darkness of that battle in the West
> Where all of high and holy dies away.

Later in the same text Buchan cites the need of the German army for recruits. They had demanded 700,000 men from Russian Poland, which deeply incensed Russia and did not mislead the Poles themselves who could not accept the situation:

> *"Non tali auxilio, nec defensoribus istis*
> *Tempes eget."*

Towards the end of the war, when most Eastern Bloc countries had capitulated, German forces were beginning to give in. Buchan commented;

> Whatever crimes she had committed in the long war were now blossoming to her hurt.

>   The Gods alone
>   Remember everlastingly; they strike
>   Remorselessly and ever like for like.
>   By their great memories the Gods are known.

'Mr Standfast'   *(1919)*

There are a couple of lines of poetry in *Mr Standfast* (1918), the third Buchan 'shocker' with Richard Hannay. Hannay learns the

> West Hielandman is no fond o' hard work. Ye ken the psalm o' the crofter.

>   O that the peats would cut themselves,
>   The fish chump on the shore,
>   And that I in my bed might lie
>   Henceforth for evermore!

Later when Blenkiron seeks to persuade Hannay to use Mary as a decoy for Ivery he asks

> What is it the poet sings?

>   White hands cling to the bridle rein,
>   Slipping the spur from the booted heel.

Near the end of the story Hannay remembers.

> A line of an old song, which had been a favourite of my father's, sang itself in my ears:

>   There's an eye that ever weeps and a fair face will be fain
>   When I ride through Annan Water wi' my bonny bands again!

'These for Remembrance' *(1919)*

This memoir of six of Buchan's close friends killed during the First World War was privately printed about June 1919. It remained unavailable to a wider public until republished in facsimile in 1987.

Buchan says of his former business partner Tommy Nelson that

He had a quick sympathy and a very tender heart in the face of

> the fierce confederate storm
> Of sorrow, baricadoed evermore
> Within the walls of cities.

When writing of Cecil Rawling he thought 'He was most akin to the best type of British private soldier', and of these he says:

> "Their shoulders held the heavens suspended,
> They stood, and earth's foundations stay,
> What God abandoned these defended,
> And saved the sum of things for pay."

'The History of the South African Forces in France' *(1920)*

At the end of the First World War Buchan was asked by General Smuts to write a history of the South African Forces. The book was published in March 1920 and includes several lines of poetry. Describing the battle at Longueval, Buchan takes inspiration from Scottish history:

> But, as at Flodden, when

> they left the darkening heath
> More desperate grew the strife of death.

'Francis and Riversale Grenfell' *(1920)*

Another privately published war memoir was a short biography of two brothers, Francis and Rivy Grenfell, whom Buchan had known before the war. The preface includes the following verse:

> Time takes them home that we loved, fair names and famous,
>   To the soft long sleep, to the broad sweet bosom of death;
> But the flower of their souls he shall not take away to shame us,
>   Nor the lips lack song for ever that now lack breath.
> For with us shall the music and perfume that die not dwell,
> Through the dead to our dead bid welcome, and we farewell.

And as an introduction to the last paragraph he gives the following lines:

> Tarry, dear cousin Suffolk!
> My soul shall thine keep company to heaven;
> Tarry, sweet soul, for mine, then fly abreast,
> As in this glorious and well-foughten field
> We kept together in our chivalry!

'Full Circle' *(1920)*

Buchan's short story about a house with a strange presence, 'Full Circle', was published in *Blackwood's Magazine* and *Atlantic Monthly* in January 1920 and later collected in *The Runagates Club* (1928). It is introduced with a short verse:

> Between the Windrush and the Colne
> I found a little house of stone —
> A little wicked house of stone.

'The Path of the King' *(1921)*

Taken from the book of this title, published during March 1921. It also appeared as a periodical in *Outward Bound* between October 1920 and October 1921.

The first tale is of a prince who, as a child, is told stories by his mother and by the maids. The maids tell the Wicking lullaby:

> "Hush thee, my bold one, a boat I will buy thee,
>   A boat and stout oars and a bright sword beside,
> A helm of red gold and a thrall to be nigh thee,
>   When fair blows the wind at the next wicking-tide."

Later another character recites to the prince:

> "Three nines of maidens ride,
> But one rides before them,
> A white maid helmed:
> From the manes the steeds shake
> Dew into the deep dales,
> Hail upon the high woods."

In another chapter Sir Walter Raleigh lies ill with a fever. The captain of his flagship, the *Destiny*, pays a visit and they discuss a recent battle and past life. Raleigh reveals,

Once I was like Kit Marlowe's Tambourlaine

> 'Threatening the world with high astounding terms,
> And scourging kingdoms with his conquering sword.'

But now the flame has died and the ashes are cold. . . .

'Huntingtower' *(1922)*

Huntingtower (1922) is the first of the trilogy centering around the adventures of a retired Glasgow grocer Dickson McCunn. McCunn considers retirement, old age and youth;

"What's a man's age? He must hurry more, that's all;
Cram in a day, what his youth took a year to hold:
When we mind labour, then only, we're too old —
What age had Methusalem when he begat Saul?"

Dickson reads the 'first fruits' of his fellow traveller John Heritage:

"Sunflowers, tall Grenadiers, ogle the roses' short-skirted ballet.
The fumes of dark sweet wine hidden in frail petals
Madden the drunkard bees."

And the poet himself sings some of his lines on the subject of evening:

"The painted gauze of the stars flutters in a fold of twilight crape,
The moon's pale leprosy sloughs the fields."

After a long discussion on the merits and demerits of poetry Dickson
McCunn and Heritage reach 'The Cruives Inn' where the poet sings:

"Thou shalt hear a song
After a while which Gods may listen to;
But place the flask upon the board and wait
Until the stranger hath allayed his thirst,
For poets, grasshoppers, and nightingales
Sing cheerily but when the throat is moist."

One of the Gorbals Die-Hards, Dougal Crombie, while waiting to storm the
castle of Huntingtower, begins

to sing, to a hymn tune, a strange ditty:

"Class-conscious we are, and class-conscious wull be
Till our fit's on the neck o' the Boorjoyzee."

Another Die-Hard, Jaikie, sings later to the tune of "Annie Laurie" another
of the 'ditties of his quondam Sunday school':

"The Boorjoys' brays are bonnie,
Too-roo-ra-roo-raloo,
But the Worrkers o' the Worrld

200

Wull gar them a' look blue,
Wull gar them a' look blue,
   And droon them in the sea,
And for bonnie Annie Laurie
   I'll lay me down and dee."

He adds

"Proley Tarians, arise!
   Wave the Red Flag to the skies,
Heed nae mair the Fat Man's lees,
   Stap them doun his throat!
Nocht to loss except our chains — "

Finally after the battle is won Heritage declaims:

"And on her lover's arm she leant,
   And round her waist she felt it fold,
And far across the hills, they went
   In that new world which is the old:
Across the hills, and far away
   Beyond their utmost purple rim,
And deep into the dying day
   The happy princess followed him."

'Midwinter's Song'   (1922)

'Midwinter's Song' was written in 1922 and appeared the following year in
Midwinter, Buchan's historical novel about Elsfield and the surrounding
area. The poem appears in *Poems Scots and English* (1936 edition).

"Diana and her darling crew
   Will pluck your fingers fine,
And lead you forth right pleasantly
   To drink the honey wine, —
To drink the honey wine, my dear,

And sup celestial air,
And dance as the young angels dance,
Ah, God that I were there!"

Midwinter opens with a young soldier Alastair MacLean meeting Amos Midwinter who sings:

"Three naked men I saw,
one to hang and one to draw,
one to feed the corbie's maw."
"Three naked men we be,
Stark aneath the blackthorn tree
Christ ha' mercy on such as we!"

Later, at the inn called the Sleeping Deer he sings Midwinter's song. When Nicholas Kyd is tried for betraying the secrets of his master, and sentenced to be banished, he states,

I'm like the old ballad:

Happy the craw
That biggs i' the Totten Shaw
And drinks o' the Water of Dye,
For nae mair may I.

Nearing the end of the story the Duchess and Alastair halt and listen to a voice, which had sung 'Diana' at the Sleeping Deer.

'O Love' the voice sang —

"O Love, they wrong thee much
That say thy sweet is bitter,
When thy rich fruit is such
As nothing can be sweeter.
Fair house of joy and bliss,
Where truest treasure is,
I do adore thee."

The voice hung on the lines for an instant in a tremor of passion. Then it continued to a falling close —

"I know thee what thou art,
I serve thee with my heart,
    And fall before thee."

Outside a tavern in Derbyshire Alastair hears fellows celebrating:

"George is magnanimous,
Subjects unanimous,
    Peace to us bring,"

Then some one started an air he knew too well:

"O Brother Sawney, hear you the news?
Twang 'em, we'll bang 'em, and
    Hang 'em up all.
An army's just coming without any shoes,
Twang 'em, we'll bang 'em, and
    Hang 'em up all."

At the end of the book Samuel Johnson meets General Oglethorpe who quotes two lines:

"One, driven by strong benevolence of soul,
Shall fly like Oglethorpe from pole to pole."

'The Last Secrets' *(1923)*

This book, published during September 1923, contains a record of some of the main achievements of early twentieth century exploration. In his Preface Buchan writes:–

There are no more unvisited forbidden cities, or unapproached high mountains, or unrecorded great rivers.

The world is disenchanted; oversoon
Must Europe send her spies through all the land.

'A History of English Literature' *(1923)*

In 1923 Buchan edited *A History of English Literature* for Nelson. The following is from Chapter 10, 'The End of the Century' which Buchan wrote himself. Discussing George Meredith Buchan adds two lines of poetry about his not being

afraid of honest laughter:

Laughter! O thou reviver of sick Earth, good for the spirit, good
For body thou! to both art wine and bread.

'Lord Minto' *(1924)*

Buchan concludes his biography of *Lord Minto*, a former Governor-General of Canada:

"Blest are those
Whose blood and judgment are so well commingled."

'The Three Hostages' *(1924)*

In his first postwar adventure Richard Hannay's Cotswold idyll is disturbed by a request from Sir Walter Bullivant, now Lord Artinswell, to find three kidnap victims. The only clue is the following poem linking the kidnappings:

"Seek where under midnight's sun
Laggard crops are hardly won; —
Where the sower casts his seed in
Furrows of the fields of Eden; —
Where beside the sacred tree
Spins the seer that cannot see."

'The Man and the Book' *(1925)*

Buchan's short life of *Sir Walter Scott, The Man and the Book*, quotes extensively from Scott's own poetry. Towards the end of the book Buchan includes some of his own lines.

The sword had been worn out by use and not by rust, and he had been faithful to his own creed —

> One crowded hour of glorious life
> Is worth an age without a name.

'The Dancing Floor' *(1926)*

The plot of Buchan's novel set on a Greek Island, *The Dancing Floor* (1926) depends on a parchment covered with Greek characters. When translated it contained a verse:

"Io, Kouros most great. I give thee hail.
Come, O Dithyrambos, Bromios come, and bring with thee
Holy hours of thy most holy spring. . . .
Then will be flung over earth immortal a garland of flowers,
Voices of song will rise among the pipes,
The Dancing Floor will be loud with the calling of crowned Semele."

Later, while crossing the valley of the Dancing Floor, Sir Edward remembers:

> "where Helicon breaks down
> In cliff to the sea. . . .
>
> Where moon-silver'd inlets
> Send far their light voice — "

'Tendebant Manus' *(1927)*

Tendebant Manus, a short story about brotherly love and included in *The Runagates Club* (1928) includes the verse:

> "Fight on, fight on," said Sir Andrew Barton.
> " 'Though I be wounded I am not slain.
> I'll lay me down and bleed a while,
>   And then I'll rise and fight again."

'Witch Wood' *(1927)*

Witch Wood (1927) is often regarded as Buchan's most profound and deeply felt novel. The Reverend David Sempill arrives in August 1644 as minister to the parish of Woodilea. The nearby Wood of Caledon intrigues him and while exploring it, he is startled by a voice singing:

> "Weary, Ovie, gang awa',
> Haste ye furth o' house an' ha',
> Ower the muir and doun the burn,
> Wearie, Ovie, ne'er return."

(This verse appeared first in *Grey Weather* within the chapter entitled 'At the Article of Death' 1899, but it differs in the second line.)

Later he meets Katrine Yester of Calidon who sings:

> *"O fontaine Bellerie,*
> *Belle fontaine chérie*
> *De nos Nymphes, quand ton eau*
> *Les cache au creux de ta source,*
> *Fuyantes le Satyreau*
> *Qui les pourchasse a la course*
> *Jusqu'au bord de ton ruisseau,*
> *Tu es la Nymphe éternelle*
> *De ma terre paternelle —"*

Later she sings:

"The King's young dochter was sitting in her window,
  Sewing at her silken seam;
She lookt out o' a bow-window,
  And she saw the leaves growing green,
    My luve;
  And she saw the leaves growing green."

  "There's comfort for the comfortless,
    And honey for the bee,
  And there's nane for me but you, my love,
    And there's nane for you but me.'

  It's love for love that I have got,
    And love for love again,
  So turn your high horse heid about
    And we will ride for hame, my love,
  And we will ride for hame."

During the inquiry into suggestions that Bessie Todd is a witch, her purported confession is read by David. It contains a spell sung by the witch when eating her 'witchcake':

  "Some lass maun gang wi' a kilted sark;
  Some priest maun preach in a thackless kirk;
  Thread maun be spun for a dead man's sark;
  A' maun be done ere the sang o' the lark."

At Woodilee 'a curious langour fell' and Amos Ritchie having said he did not like it quoted a verse his grannie had of 'auld Thomas the Rhymer':

  "A Yule wi'out snaws,
  A Januar' wi' haws,
  Bring the deid thraws."

At the end of the story fragments of Katrine's songs come back to David:

  "There's comfort for the comfortless
  And honey for the bee . . ."

'The Runagates Club' *(1928)*

In the Preface to this his only volume of postwar short stories Buchan describes the atmosphere in a London private club, and the talk therein as

like that of Praed's Vicar,

> slipped from politics to puns,
> And passed from Mahomet to Moses.

'Montrose' *(1928)*

Apart from the dedicatory poem only one verse appears to be by Buchan himself. When recounting the history of the first covenant wars it is said:

One form of violence was to be matched by another.

> The Gods alone
> Remember everlastingly; they strike
> Remorselessly, and ever like for like.
> By their great memories the Gods are known.

'Pierce the Piper's Song' *(1929)*

Taken from *The Blanket Of The Dark* (1931). It appears under this title in *Poems Scots and English* (1936 edition), where it is dated 1929.

> "Worm at my heart and fever in my head —
> There is no peace for any but the dead.
> Only the dead are beautiful and free.
> *Mortis cupiditas captavit me.*"

'Sabine's Song' *(1929)*

Likewise taken from *The Blanket Of The Dark* (1931). It appears under this
title in *Poems Scots and English* (1936 edition), where it is dated 1929.

> "Summer has come with love to town,
> Throstle in bush and lark on down
>   Merrily tell their tale O.
>   Folk that pine
>   Now drink sunshine
>   More strong than winter's ale O.
> Sweet mistress, why so pale O?
>   I hie to thee
>   As river to sea
> When the deer draw to the dale O."

'The Courts of the Morning' *(1929)*

The Courts of the Morning (1929) was originally to have been called '*Far
Arabia*' and Sandy quotes some apposite lines at the beginning of the novel:

> He is crazed by the spell of far Arabia,
> It has stolen my mind away.

'The Kirk in Scotland' *(1930)*

In the opening chapter Buchan, when writing about the Mediaeval Church,
quotes an old song:

> That all the world shall see
> There's nane right but we,
> The men of the auld Scottish nation.

Later in the chapter discussing The Union he gives this verse:

Why else was the pause prolonged but that
singing might issue thence?
Why rushed the discords in but that
harmony should be prized?

In the last chapter on the future of the Church of Scotland he writes:

wide
And tranquil, from whose floor the new-bathed stars
Emerge and shine upon the Aral sea.

'*The Blanket of the Dark*' *(1931)*

The Blanket of the Dark (1931) centres around a clerk Peter Pentecost who
learns he is the rightful claimant to the English throne. He is introduced to
Madge Littlemouse, who is learned in the 'old wisdom' but who

never dried up the ewes or the kine with the charm —

Hare's milk and mare's milk,
And all the beasts that bears milk
Come ye to me . . .

Peter later meets the 'Parliament of Beggars' in the Greenwood, where
Pierce the piper plays a tune on his fiddle and sings:

"Peter sat at Heaven's gate
Beeking in the sun,
While the souls came up the stair
Limping every one,
Like the weary homing rooks
When the day is done."

John Naps commands him to put more mirth into his music, and
he obeys with a song:

"When is the time to drink with a friend?
When is it meetest thy money to spend?

O now, now, now,
O now, now, now.

"When should a man fill his belly with meat
Cool his hot throat and anoint his sore feet?
O now, now, now.

"When are most honied the lips of a lass?
When tastes the sweetest the foam on the glass?
O now, now, now."

Later Pierce is asked to 'give us a stave': (see 'Pierce the Piper's Song'
above.)
Sabine Beauforest is introduced to Peter and sings a song: (see
'Sabine's Song', above.)
Then the man, named as the 'gospeller' recites a few lines:

"Christ crucified
For thy wounds wide
Us commons guide
Which pilgrims be!"

Darking quotes a country rhyme:

"The Cat, the Rat, and Lovell our dog
Ruled all England under the Hog."

A line of 'some wandering poet' comes into Peters' head:

"O blandos oculos et inquietos!"

and he searches his memory for more:

*"Illic et Venus et leves Amores
Atque ipso in medio sedet Voluptas."*

He then tries to turn the verse into his own tongue:

"For there dwells Venus, and the tiny Loves,
And in their midst Delight."

Later he remembers some lines of Boethius:

211

"Ite nunc fortes ubi celsa magni
Ducit exempli via.'

He sings it aloud to the empty wolds:

"Go forth, ye brave, on the high road
Where honour calls to honour's wars;
Strip from your back the craven load;
Go spurn the earth and win the stars."

'Sir Walter Scott' *(1932)*

Buchan includes four of his own verses in his 1932 life of Sir Walter Scott.
He describes Scott's retirement from Clerkship of the Court,

. . . but, there was not to be that quiet evening, that

old age, serene and bright
And lovely as a Lapland night,

which his strenuous life deserved.

Outlining Scott's Vision of Life,

. . . It [the novel] must posses that "stellar and undiminishable
somthing" which can

tease us out of thought,
As doth eternity.

Later on 'The Man and Worldliness' Buchan writes,

The dweller in it could not be one of those

who rest not; who think long
Till they discern as from a hill
At the sun's hour of morning song,
Known of souls only, and those souls free,
The sacred spaces of the sea.

212

In the section 'His Rule of Life' he writes,

> He was above all things a countryman, who knew and honoured the peasant; of the proletariat in towns, and

> the fierce confederate storm
> Of sorrow barricadoed evermore
> Within the walls of cities,

'A Prince of the Captivity'   *(1933)*

The dedication in this book, published in July 1933, is to Edward Stephen Harkness, the founder of The Pilgrim Trust. The following verse appears:

> "As when a Prince
> Of dispers'd Israel, chosen in the shade,
> Rules by no canon save his inward light,
> And knows no pageant save the pipes and shawms
> Of his proud spirit."

In Book I the central character Adam Melfort is cited as having been 'a voracious reader of poetry':

> "Come ill, come well, the cross, the crown,
>   The rainbow or the thunder —
> I fling my soul and body down
>   For God to plough them under."

'The Free Fishers' *(1934)*

Anthony Lammas, 'a licensed minister of the Kirk and a professor in the University of St Andrews', is marching along the road whistling the tune of 'Dunbarton's Drums', the words of which are:

> "Dunbarton's drums are bonnie O —
> I'll leave a' my friends and my daddie O —
> I'll bide nae mair at hame, but I'll follow wi' the drum,
> And whenever it beats I'll be ready O."

The Free Fishers are a secret society mainly consisting of, but not all, sea-faring folk. When dining they were 'piped to meat by a bosun's whistle', and they said the Fisher's Grace, which begins:

> "For flukes and partans, cakes and ale,
> Salty beef and seein' kale — "

and concludes 'with a petition for the same mercies at the next meeting'.

Lammas recognises the voice of John Kinloch and the song he sings

> 'Katie Beardie had a coo,
> A' black aboot the moo, —
> Wasna yon a denty coo? —
> Dance, Katie Beardie.'

John Kinloch is introduced to Sir Turnour Wyse, who asks 'Is he perhaps a Scotch cousin?', and is given in reply 'Oh no. Only a childhood's friend. Long ago we played together.'

'I see.' said Sir Turnour, 'As your Scotch poet sings,

> We two have paddled in the burn.'

[This is a line from John Buchan's own poem 'Fisher Jamie']

At the entrance to Hungrygrain the carriage driven by Mr Niven is stopped by three men. Mr Dott, the passenger, is told there is no lady at the house, and asks 'Where is she' and the reply:

214

"Maybe
Up the mossy mountain
And down the dowie glen?"

Later Lammas, in a mood of high exhilaration, wants to declaim poetry —

"Rumoresque senum severiorum
Omnes unius aestimemus assis. . . ."

Mr Dott is accused by Bob Muschat 'of a purpose of love and not of greed'.
Bob had a verse of a wicked song:

"A bonny may went out one day
Some fresh fish for to buy,
An' there she spied a wee toun-clerk,
An' he followed her speedily —
Ricky doo dum dae, doo dum dae,
Ricky dicky doo dum dae."

At the Roman Urn Inn, Mr Winfortune is singing to the guests a slow sad
rhythm:

"It's up and farewell unto you, Spanish ladies,
It's up and farewell to you, ladies of Spain,
For we are a-sailing beyond the bar of Cadiz,
And never, no never, we'll come back to you again."

'Oliver Cromwell' *(1934)*

In his biography of Cromwell Buchan has the following lines when analy-
sing puritanism:

Such as thou has solemnly elected,
With gifts and graces eminently adorned,
To some great work, thy glory,
And people's safety.

Later in the biography when it is suggested Cromwell was aiming at the throne:

> "Thou art the King of our New State
> And worthy to undoe us."

Though 'still a monarchist but Charles was impossible as king' Cromwell is faced with decision:

> "Causeless they like a bird have chased me;
> Behold, O Lord, look down from heaven and see,
> Thou that hearest prisoners' prayers, hear me!
>   Never was grief like mine."

Of Ormonde he says,

> he had shown infinite patience and fortitude,
>
> > Doing the king's work all the dim day long.

And of Blake,

> who kept his place on the Spanish Coasts during the winter . . .
>
> > Others may use the ocean as their road,
> > Only the English make it their abode,
> > Whose ready sails with every wind can fly,
> > And make a covenant with th' inconstant sky;
> > Our oaks secure as if they there took root,
> > We tread on billows with a steady foot.

After the death of Oliver Cromwell, Buchan says,

> Already a new realism was being born, a prosaic and critical spirit—
>
> > Thy wars brought nothing about,
> >   Thy Lovers were all untrue.
> > 'Tis well an Old Age is out,
> >   And time to begin a New.

Yet even the dullest understood that a great thing had gone from the world

'The King's Grace' *(1935)*

In the prologue of this book, written to mark the twenty-fifth Jubilee of his reign, Buchan says of King George, and of kings in general:

> His duty is not to act but to be, to represent the ultimate sanctities of the land which endure behind passing fevers and bewilderments: like Time,
>
> > "who in the twilight comes to mend
> > All the fantastic day's caprice."

Later when discussing the Great War Buchan writes:

> Britain launched her little army into the void with the anxiety with which men and nations face something which is new in their experience but on which hang mighty issues
>
> > Far other is this battle in the west,
> > Whereto we move, than when we strove in youth
> > And break the petty kings.

and,

> > Which softness' self, is yet the stuff
> > To hold fast where a steel chain snaps.

When peace comes:

> > Tiny pleasures occupy the place
> > Of glories and of duties: as the feet
> > Of fabled fairies, when the sun goes down,
> > Trip o'er the grass where wrestlers strove by day.

The true spirit of peace-making had not yet been generated, and the words of Bernard of Marlaix haunted many minds:

> *Pax erit omnibus unica, sed quibus? Immaculatis,*
> *Pectore mitibus, ordine stantibus, ore sacratis.*

At the conclusion of the second epilogue (in the reissued book printed during February 1936) John Buchan quotes Carlyle's phrase about Scott, 'no

217

sounder piece of manhood was fashioned in our generation, for he had in him both warmth and light'. And adds one of his favourite expressions:

"Blest are those
Whose blood and judgment are so well commingled"

'The House of the Four Winds' *(1935)*

Ranald Glynde is talking with John Galt (Jaikie of the late, Gorbals Die-Hards) about Alison Westwater. He says

I have been writing verses in her honour in the only tongue in which a goddess should be hymned.

Alison, bella puella candida,
Quae bene superas lac et lilium
Album, quae simul rosam rubidam
Aut expolitum ebur Indicum,
Pande, puella, pande capillulos
Flavos, lucentes ut aurum nitidum.

'The Island of Sheep' *(1936)*

The Island of Sheep (1936), Richard Hannay's last adventure has only one verse. Hannay is haunted by a

ridiculous sailor's rhyme:

"Take care, beware
The Bight of Benin —
One comes out
Though forty go in."

'Medicine I'   *(1936)*

Taken from *Canadian Occasions* (1940), a collection of Buchan's Canadian speeches. The paper was read to the Ontario Medical Association on 27 May 1936. Talking of Lord Lister in his old age, John Buchan writes:

It was the face of a conqueror, of a happy warrior who

> Born to walk in company with pain
> And fear and blood-shed, miserable train,
> Turns his necessity to glorious gain.

'Return to Masterpieces'   *(1937)*

Another essay from *Canadian Occasions* (1940). The paper was read to the Canadian Authors Association on 24 November 1937. Buchan shows his gift for pastiche in rewriting for a Holywood film, 'O Mistress Mine':

> Huh! Sweetie, where you gettin' to?
> Your big boy's here and pettin' you,
>   And he's the guy that rings the bell.
> Say, kid, quit hikin' and sit nice,
> For shakin' feet don't cut no ice,
>   The goopiest mutt can tell.

'Augustus'   *(1937)*

In his biography of *Augustus* he says of Lepidus:

> a slight, unmeritable man
> Meet to be sent on errands.

and of Cleopatra:

Imperishable fire under the boughs
Of chrysoberyl and beryl and chrysolite,
And chrysoprase and ruby and sardonyx.

Later, when describing Rome, he says:

Confusae sonus urbis et inlaetabile murmur.

'Memory Hold the Door'   *(1940)*

In this, his autobiography, Buchan says his study of the classics was:

based on the crystalline sea
of truth and its eternity.

Describing his days at Oxford, he writes:

bright and intricate device
Of days and seasons.

and when recounting his experiences in South Africa he says:

Lo! for there among the flowers and grasses
Only the mightier movement sounds and passes;
Only wind and rivers,
Life and death.

and:

I was all ear
And took in strains that might create a soul
Under the ribs of death.

Having moved to Elsfield he found that he loved

with equal mind
The southern sun, the northern wind,

> The lilied lowland watermead,
> And the grey hills that cradle the Tweed;

After entering Parliament in 1927 he claimed to be concerned for the future of democracy:

> The high post-war visions had gone, and the prevalent mood was, at the best, a stoical resolution.
>
> > Life still
> > Leaves human efforts scope.
> > But, since life teems with ill,
> > Nurse no extravagant hope;
> > Because thou must not dream, thou need'st not then despair.

Writing about his brother William's death:

> There his life slowly ebbed:
>
> > through long days of labouring breath
> > He watched the world grow small and far
> > And met the constant eyes of death,
> > And haply knew how kind they are.

Of his own middle life and

> memories of a happy past are in themselves a solid possession;
>
> > Is it so small a thing
> > To have enjoy'd the sun,
> > To have lived light in the spring?

He writes of 'lowland streams' which he liked best when the turf is

> just beginning to green after the winter:
>
> > A month before the month of May,
> > And the spring comes slowly up this way

In the case of fishing itself he writes of seeing

> the bursting fly-books and tackle boxes of my friends I do not envy

them:

> Perish the wish, for inly satisfied,
> Above their pomps I hold my ragged pride.

He gives 'a little piscatorial eclogue which I used to hear repeated in my youth, but the source of which I have never been able to trace.' It is entitled 'Juvenus and Piscator', and it is worthy of repetition here;

Juv. Canny Fisher Jamie, comin' hame at e'en,
Canny Fisher Jamie, whaur hae ye been?

Pisc. Mony lang miles, laddie, ower the Kips sae green.

Juv. Fishin' Leithen Water?

Pisc.   Nay, laddie, nay,
Just a wee burnie rinnin' doun a brae,
Fishin' a wee burnie bigger than a sheugh.

Juv Gat ye mony troots, Jamie?

Pisc.   I gat eneugh —
Eneugh to buy my baccy, snuff, and pickle tea,
And lea' me tippence for a gill, and that's eneugh for me.

ॐ ॐ ॐ

222

Glossary

a' all
aboon/abune above/over
aboot about
ae one
ahint behind
aiblins perhaps
ain own
aince once
aiten oaten
alang along
amang among
ane one
anither another
atween between
aucht anything
auchteen eighteen
auld old
auldfarrant oldfashioned
awa away

bade bid
bannocks pancakes
bairn child
bairnliest babiest
baith both
bauchled distorted
bauks untilled land
bauld bold
bawbee halfpenny
bawl shout
bawsened white faced
begood begun
belchin' preaching
ben through
beuk book
bicker drinking cup
bickerin' arguing
biddin's orders
bield shelter
birk birch
blae blue
blate shy
blaw blow
bleeze blaze

bluid blood
brae hill
braid broad
braw fine
braxy diseased
breeks trousers
broo brow
bucht sheep pen
buid bid
buits boots
bund bond/bound
burnie brook
buskit dressed
busses bushes
bye beside/near
byliff bailiff

ca' call
ca'ed called
canna cannot
canty lively
carle old man
cauld cold
chappin knocking
chaumer chamber
cheild boy
chuckies chickens
claes clothes
clamjamfried worthless
clart/y dirt/y
claught clutched
clinkit struck
cockit heaped
coorts courts
coup upset
couthy kindly
crackin' chatting
craw crow/boast
creashy greasy
crood crowd
croun crown
crously briskly
cuif fool
cuisten cast

223

cundies conduits

dacent decent
dae do
dander stroll
daunder saunter
daured dared
dawf remove
delve dig
denty dainty
ding knock
dochter daughter
Dod george
doo dove/pidgeon
doots doubts
doucely quiet
doun down
dowie sad
driech/est dull/est
drooned drowned
dwaibly feeble

een eyes
eneuch enough
errin' errant
ettle attempt

faes foes
farles oatcakes
fauld fold
faun fallen
fauts faults
ferlie strange
feucht fight
fleechin' flattering
fleein' flying
floo'rs flowers
flytit scolded
frae from
freend friend
frem't foreign
fricht fright
fan when
furthy frank

gaed went

gait stride
gangs goes
garred made
gaucy plump
ghaist ghost
gie/n give/n
glaikit stupid
glaury muddy
gleg horsefly
gleg's bright
gloomin' frowning
glower glare
glumchin looking sad
goud gold
gowans daisies
gowk fool
greetin' crying
grue ice
grumblin' grumbling
grund ground
guddlin' tickling trout
guid good

hae have
hain/in's enclose/ures
hairst harvest
hale whole
halms stalks/shaws
hame home
happit wrapped
haughlands highlands
heid head
heinchin chicken
hert heart
heuchs exclamations
hirsel collection
hoddit held
hoodie craws black head crows
howkin' digging
hunkerin' squatting

ilka every
ither other

jee stir
jimped leaped
jouked ducked

kent known
kenned knew
kep cap
kets carrion
kittle tickle
kinle light
kye cattle

lauchin' laughing
lee lie
lickit defeated
licht light
loon boy
Losh Lord
loup leap
louse free
lowe flame

mair more
mairrit married
maist most
makkers poets
maud plaid
maukit infested
maun must
massy massive
meuse honour
micht might
midden dung heap
misdoot misdoubt
mools moles
mou mouth
muckle much/great

nae no
nane none
neebors neighbours
niffer barter/haggle
nieves fists
nocht nothing
nou now

'oo wool
ower over
orra odd

paiks strikes/pokes

pairt part
parritch porridge
piked gathered
plock third of penny
ploom plum
ploos ploughs
plowtered waded
poke grope
pooches pockets/pouches
poopits pulpits
poether powder
puir poor
puirtith poverty

quate quiet

rade afraid
rape rope
raws rows
reddin' clearing
reid read
richt right
roopy hoarsely
rauk fag
roup auction
rows rolls

sae so
sair sore
saunts saints
scabbit scabbed
scaith scathe
scaud scald
schauchled shackled
schauchlin' shaking
sel self
shairn/y cows dung/daubed in
shouther shoulder
shilpit pale
siccan such
siller silver
sin since
skeely skilled
skelped smacked
skreich break of day
snoddit tidied
snoukin' to smell as a dog
snoutit snouted

225

spainin weaning
spak spoke
speir ask
speldered split
splore explore
staig stag
staucherin' staggering
stausome disgusting
steeked latched
stench strong
stert/it start/ed
stievest stiffest
stirk cow
stramash uproar
straucht straight
sudna should not
swirds swords

tackets tacks
taen taken
tak take
tautit matted
tawmont two months
tentier careful
teuch tough
thack thatch
thegither together
thocht thought
thole bear
thrall worry
thrang stubborn
thrapple throat
threep/it whistle/d
thristles thistles
tine lose
tippeny two pence
toddy whisky

toom empty
toun town
traivelled travelled
trig/s trim/tidy
tups rams
twae two

unco extraordinarily
unction auction

wae/fu' woe/ful
walie feeble
wame belly/womb
wanchancy unlucky
warstled wrestled
wauf wave
wauks wakens
wean child
wecht weight
whae who
whaup curlew
whaur where
whase whose
whilk which
wight creature
wrocht worked

yaird yard
yammerin' whining
ye you
yestreen yesterday
yett gate
yill ale
yin one
yon that/yonder
yowe cattle

Bibliography

Blanchard, Robert G. *The First Editions of John Buchan*. Archon Books, 1981.

Daniell, David. *The Interpreter's House*. Thomas Nelson & Sons, 1975.

Lownie, Andrew. *John Buchan The Presbyterian Cavalier*. Constable, 1995.

Lownie, Andrew (ed). *John Buchan: The Complete Short Stories* vols 1–3. Thistle, 1996.

Smith, Janet Adam. *John Buchan, A Biography*. Rupert Hart Davies, 1965. *John Buchan and his World*. Thames and Hudson, 1979.

Index of Poem Titles

Index of First Lines